Musical Instruments for Children

Musical Instruments
for Children

choosing what's right for your child

Richard Crozier

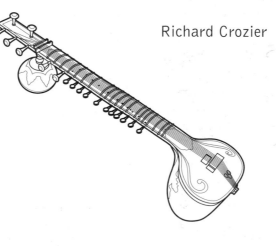

hamlyn

First published in Great Britain in 2007 by
Hamlyn, a division of Octopus Publishing Group Ltd
2–4 Heron Quays, London E14 4JP

Copyright © Octopus Publishing Group Ltd 2007

Distributed in the United States and Canada by
Sterling Publishing Co., Inc.
387 Park Avenue South, New York, NY 10016-8810

ISBN-13: 978-0-600-61571-2
ISBN-10: 0-600-61571-5

A CIP catalogue record for this book is available
from the British Library.

Printed and bound in China

10 9 8 7 6 5 4 3 2 1

As musical instruments vary according to
manufacturer and model, the illustrations in
this book are intended only as a reference and a
guide to the reader and are not shown to scale. For
more accurate information on each instrument, refer
to an appropriate music teacher or musical
instrument retailer.

CONTENTS

INTRODUCTION

Learning to play a musical instrument is fun! The learning process should be as enjoyable as participating in music-making with friends, which can bring great pleasure and lead to the establishment of strong friendship bonds and happy lifelong memories. A small number of learners go on to become professional musicians. Others play as a rewarding pastime, or join an ensemble, band or orchestra and enjoy sociable music-making for many years to come. (As a twenty-year-old I played in bands and orchestras alongside musicians in their 80s.) And for most of us, playing an instrument becomes a way to develop a deeper understanding of music. When we can play an instrument, we better appreciate the creative process of making music and the acts of composition and performance; when we listen to music, we engage with it in an enhanced way.

Learning to play a musical instrument well is really hard work. It's a good idea to persevere with lessons for 8–12 months, or two to three school terms, to get to know whether the instrument is right for you. Even if it isn't, there is no shame in moving on to a different instrument. Only in this way will you find exactly the right match. The rewards of learning to play far outweigh the difficulties. I hope you will have as much fun learning as I have had teaching and playing.

Richard Crozier

HOW TO USE THIS BOOK

This book is designed for parents, carers, teachers and children. It aims to help you choose a musical instrument children will enjoy learning and that suits them as beginners. It is also an invaluable source of information for the growing number of adult learners who wish to take up an instrument, perhaps having missed the opportunity in their childhood or teenage years.

In Part 1 (see pages 8–37) you will find general advice and background information on the process of learning a musical instrument, including an explanation of different learning styles and suggested ways to choose a teacher. To focus your thinking, there are pointers to instruments that might best suit learners of various ages, temperaments, personalities, learning styles and preferred listening. The author answers every parent's most frequently asked questions and offers a resources section packed with the website addresses of invaluable music education organizations.

Part 2 (see pages 38-113) provides detailed descriptions of all the most commonly taught musical instruments, from cornet and piano to clarinet and flute, arranged in musical families, such as woodwind, brass and percussion. It also highlights more unusual choices, such as steel pans, tabla, folk harp and fiddle, to appeal to the growing number of learners inspired to explore the music of non-Western cultures and traditional genres. For each instrument you will find a summary of how it works and is taught, the ease with which a sound can be produced and its repertoire of music. Also detailed are personal attributes that make success on the instrument more likely, plus information on practical matters: how much space you need at home and in the car, the price of new and second-hand instruments, running and maintenance costs. Parents may be relieved to find information on likely noise levels during practice sessions – an important factor when considering electric guitar or bagpipes! If your child has already expressed keen interest in a particular instrument, turn straight to the pages that describe that instrument. If all options are still open, use the questions pages 32–37 to help you make a more informed choice.

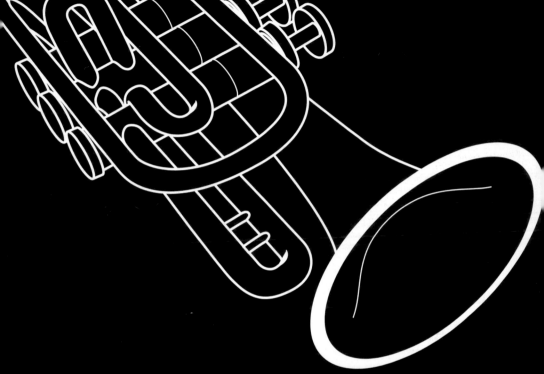

PART ONE

SO YOU WANT TO PLAY AN INSTRUMENT?

Learning to play music on an instrument is more enjoyable if the teaching style as well as the instrument suit the learner. This chapter will help you identify what to look out for in a teacher and how to choose a method of learning that reflects your child's unique personality, temperament and range of skills.

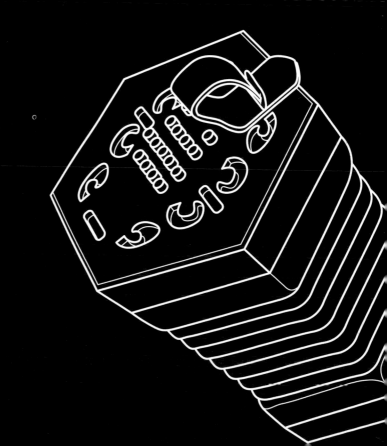

WHAT IT TAKES

WHY LEARN AN INSTRUMENT?

Playing, composing and listening to music are more than enjoyable activities. There is substantial evidence to show that participating in music-making, no matter how briefly, helps develop a range of positive and transferable skills, including cooperation, concentration, listening, coordination and fine motor skills; it even helps establish friendship groups. Learning an instrument encourages children to develop across all learning styles as they read and obey instructions, write examination answers and respond to visual signals.

What is music teaching?

In the past, learning music often meant learning about music. It can be easier for teachers to teach factual information about composers, pieces of music, musical notation and instruments than to make music, and in one sense easier for children to learn facts and be tested on whether they have remembered them rather than to put musical ideas into action. But today, many music teachers take the view that music itself does not exist. It is no more than vibrating air or strings or electronically generated sound, and so the only way to learn about it is to compose, create or listen to it. That way, a child finds out what music is made of, rather than merely learning facts about it.

Children pick up a great deal about music by learning to make and control sounds on an instrument, without wanting, or being able, to be the greatest performer on that instrument. Effective instrumental teachers teach music through the instrument, rather than just teaching the instrument itself.

What is playing music?

Ask children if they play a musical instrument and often they reply, 'Yes', meaning they enjoy making sounds on that instrument. Ask the same question to a professional musician and the answer 'Yes' means he or she has complete control and mastery over all the sounds the instrument can make. Learning to play an instrument is a journey from simply making sounds to acquiring control over sound and tone production, finding fluency as a performer and, in many cases, reading musical notation. Not everyone completes the journey, but almost all children benefit from travelling even a small part of the way.

When to begin learning

It it is never too late to begin, but of the number of school children in the population aged 5–16, the number learning to play a instrument at any one time is relatively small (in the order of 10 per cent in the UK). That percentage increases significantly in the 8–12 year age bracket, because this is the age at which children are most likely to show interest in, and most likely to gain success from, instrumental learning. It is vital that the child can hold or manipulate the instrument comfortably.

STARTING OUT

In many respects it doesn't matter which instrument you start to learn and when in life. Rather than obsessing about choosing a particular instrument, it can be as helpful to focus first on the child and his or her personality. Research evidence reveals that individuals with certain temperaments are more likely to be suited to particular instruments. Anecdotal evidence suggests that if you have a boisterous, noisy child and are hoping that a spell of learning an instrument associated with peaceful musical performance will help calm him or her it is unlikely to pay dividends. It is more realistic to start from a knowledge of whether your child is likely to persevere with a task, how consistently he applies himself to work, and what type of music and sounds he enjoys.

Begin with the child

Balance an understanding of your child's personality and temperament with her immediate, instinctive response to an instrument. For example, a child with poor coordination is likely to find playing the violin difficult, but if she really wants to learn and is fascinated by the instrument's sound and feel, it is better that she has the opportunity to find out for herself whether the violin really is the instrument for her. In Part 2 (see pages 38–113) you will find an at-a-glance analysis of each instrument, detailing its weight and size, ease of learning and the temperament it best suits. Use the information to assess the suitability of instruments your child is drawn to.

Special educational needs

There are no grounds for excluding any child from learning to play a musical instrument. If you think your child's needs may be different from the majority of others, take advice from your school or local music service on the suitability of an instrument and the relative difficulty of mastering it. Instrumental teachers working in schools have access to special educational needs coordinators. Most private teachers, even those with limited experience of working with children with special educational needs, are open to exploring how things can be made to work. Learning to play an instrument may have a therapeutic benefit, but don't confuse it with music therapy, which has a different purpose.

Does the child want to learn?

If left to their own devices, some children never consider learning to play a musical instrument. For others, the idea comes naturally, perhaps stimulated by seeing or hearing instruments at school, on screen or in the home. Parents who never took up an opportunity to learn, or dropped lessons, may project their own regrets on to children. Though it's impossible to give a general prescription to suit every family, try to follow a child's wishes and only force learning an instrument if you are willing to see it through in every respect. Children are unlikely to flourish as learners if forced to learn, and may even start playing unmusically to avoid lessons or practice sessions. Negativity brings no benefits. If a child doesn't want to learn, it is best to wait and see if he has a change of mind. Offer opportunities for learning, but don't force the issue. Simply providing a supportive and encouraging atmosphere in which to learn to play brings the best hope of success and the strongest likelihood of children developing a lifelong love of music across genres and styles. Strengthen this by being a role model of musical activity yourself, by singing, playing or listening.

MUSIC-MAKING SKILLS

Playing a musical instrument well involves multi-tasking, bringing together a complex set of skills. Pupils have to be able to listen to themselves (and sometimes others players too), make and control sounds, pay attention to pulse, rhythm, dynamics and phrasing, and probably read music, too. Teachers at school should be able to tell you if your child understands pulse, can sing back a note and hold a melodic line. Some children find these skills come so naturally that on hearing them play it can be hard to believe they have picked up an instrument for the first time. Others find certain techniques difficult to pick up, and a few children find the entire learning process challenging. An effective teacher uses a range of strategies to encourage children who find some skills difficult and helps them persevere to overcome challenges. Showing an interest in music is not the same as having ability, just as testing innate ability is not a certain pointer to future success.

Natural rhythm

The terms 'rhythm', 'pulse' and 'beat' are often used incorrectly. To establish which instrument might suit your child, it's worth getting your head around them. Most pieces of music have a pulse, much like the pulse of a living creature. If we run around the pulse speeds up, then gradually slows as we recover and rest. Most pieces of music have a steady pulse that may be at a quick tempo or a slower one. It is the pulse, not the rhythm, that we march or tap feet to. In many sorts of music pulse is referred to as the beat. Rhythmic patterns overlay the pulse and some learners find it easy to maintain a steady pulse and play differing rhythms against it. We might say that they have a natural sense of rhythm. Other beginners find this aspect of learning more difficult. A good teacher helps a learner through this difficulty.

Perfect pitch

A few people are born with 'perfect pitch': they are able to give a sound its musical pitch name on hearing it played or sung, and can hear a note and immediately sing it back confidently and accurately. This brings advantages in certain areas of musical learning. A child with perfect pitch is likely to show an aptitude for music and one view states that it is this child who should be given musical opportunities. Other children find judging pitch difficult, getting it right sometimes but inconsistently. Another point of view says that these are the very children who should be given most opportunities to improve their skills. More important is to take into account what the child wants to do.

THE JOY OF SINGING

STARTING WITH THE VOICE

The focus of this book is on learning to play a musical instrument. But almost everyone begins learning music by working with their own instrument – the singing voice. Singing is the cheapest, most readily available music-making opportunity for the majority of people, and it is one of the most pleasurable of musical activities; indeed it enhances health, because the very act of singing encourages the brain to release endorphins, the body's natural painkillers and mood enhancers. Singing is an excellent way to develop breathing, posture, self-esteem, pulse and rhythm among other qualities vital to instrumental lessons. It also enhances aural perception, which lies at the heart of music-making: the best instrumentalists and singers listen carefully to the sounds they make and are acutely aware of imperfections in tone, timbre, pitch and dynamics. Singing alone or in a well-directed group of any kind brings immense satisfaction. See it as a stepping stone to help children decide if they want to take a greater interest in music and move on to learn an instrument.

First steps

All children should have the opportunity to sing at school, either with classmates as part of the music curriculum, or by joining a choir. Sadly, singing is less common-place in schools than it used to be, and the desire to imitate styles of vocalization in popular music means many children never learn to sing properly or develop their full vocal range. Make the most of every opportunity for your child to sing, whether with a formally rehearsed choir tackling a serious repertoire or in a school vocal ensemble, church choir (often keen to recruit new members) or chorus of an amateur dramatic group, which offers the added attraction of providing stage experience in shows and musicals.

Moving on to lessons

Younger children are likely to benefit more from singing in a choir or vocal ensemble than having individual lessons. When considering individual lessons for older children, look for a teacher who understands the needs of a child's voice at different ages. Great care should be taken when nurturing young voices. It is possible to inflict lifelong damage by demanding that a young voice does things for which it is not ready. If you had negative singing experiences as a child – perhaps you were asked not to sing in class because of difficulty pitching notes – try not to pass on your anxieties. So called 'tone deafness' is extremely rare, but the condition this term is used to describe is not uncommon and an experienced trainer can help learners overcome the problem.

LEARNING TO PLAY

HOW DOES A CHILD LEARN?

All individuals, of any age, have a preferred way of learning, even if they are
unaware of or unable to articulate it.
There are no rights and wrongs; different
individuals simply learn in different ways.
You and your child know how he learns
best, and the most effective teacher is one
who relates to these needs. A good
teacher identifies a pupil's preferred
learning style and varies her teaching
style to engage with it. Less effective
teachers treat all learners in the same way.
Think back to your own school days:
which lessons did you enjoy? Which were
less memorable? Chances are the ones
you enjoyed catered better for your
learning needs.

Understanding styles of learning

In order to understand how your child
learns, it helps to identify three approach-
es to learning identified by one school of
educational thought – auditory, visual
and kinaesthetic. Auditory learners prefer
to hear instructions; visual learners favour
written or drawn communication; kinaesthetic learners like to do and find out.
Think about which best describes your
child's approach. Happily, learning and
performing music often combine all
three. The manipulation of the instrument associates certain movements with
certain sounds, which suits kinaesthetic
learners. In turn, these sounds become
associated with images on the page or
musical notation, which pleases auditory
and visual learners. Some pupils prefer to
process information before attempting
something practical, whereas others like
to start an activity straight away.
Learning an instrument offers opportunities for both.

EXPLORING DIFFERENT STYLES

It is possible to learn to play an instrument and focus exclusively on one musical style and way of learning. For
example, many electric guitarists are
inspired to learn to play by hearing, and
perhaps watching, a well-known player.
Their sole ambition is to imitate their
idol's sound, and so they practise and

practise until they eventually achieve success with one piece. They progress to the next piece and so on, consolidating technique in a slow, but effective way, which usually includes memorizing music of one style aurally. Teachers of other instruments adopt a more 'classical' approach to learning, particularly for players who spend time in bands, ensembles and orchestras. Here, the acquisition and development of technique goes hand-in-hand with an emphasis on learning how to read 'classical' music. Both teaching and learning strategies are valid.

Effective teachers develop their own curriculum and should be able to articulate their plans for a learner's musical development to parents and child. Children, especially younger pupils, are usually willing to be guided by their teacher, and so their musical diet is controlled largely by the teacher. Parents may care to check that the diet is not too narrow. For example, focusing exclusively on an examination syllabus is unlikely to be desirable, since part of the process of learning to play an instrument is learning to understand a variety of compositional and performance styles. A broad understanding provides a secure basis for in-depth study in a more specialized area later on.

Playing together

For many pupils, playing as a part of an ensemble is an essential component of the learning process. The ensemble might be an orchestra or big band, a string or wind group, a brass band or jazz ensemble, a percussion group or clarinet choir, a string quartet, brass quintet or rock group. Most children learning to play an instrument

find combining individual or small group tuition with the opportunity to play in a larger group each week is the most effective way of developing a secure instrumental technique, musical understanding and musicianship. It can also broaden their exposure to music of different styles.

The importance of motivation

In order to learn, students usually need a motivation or stimulus. They may be motivated by observing peers achieve, by rewards, by being coerced or they can want to learn from within. Intrinsic motivation – really wanting to do it – is the most powerful form of motivation, and often, with children, the most elusive to sustain. Part of the process of growing up is discovering new things, being drawn to them, and then, just as suddenly, leaving them for the next new thing. When learning an instrument this isn't helpful. Part of the job of a teacher, supported by parents, is to maintain motivation as well as perseverance, independence and skill acquisition, particularly through more difficult times.

TEACHERS & TEACHING

WHAT MAKES A SUCCESSFUL TEACHER?

An effective music teacher motivates learners with a mixture of inspiration, understanding, efficiency and a secure knowledge of all aspects of music. She covers a broad sweep of musical styles and uses a wide range of teaching strategies to engage interest. Successful teachers plan the learning and pace of delivery to meet the needs and interests of each learner, rather than following a set series of activities. They put music at the heart of a lesson and keep records on individual pupils' progress. The skill of a teacher comes in striking a balance between providing essential instruction and allowing the learner freedom to explore and experiment with the instrument, sounds and music. At one extreme this could mean dictating everything the learner must do; at the other allowing a learner to choose which pieces to learn. When the two extremes are balanced, the learner makes progress because he is motivated by the reward of success and the intrigue of achieving something new.

Key teaching methods

A good teacher uses a blend of three strategies: instruction, encounter and teaching. In the first, the learner has a clearly defined outcome and succeeds by carrying out instructed activities. Instrumental teaching sometimes focuses on instruction, emphasizing right and wrong ways of doing things.

At the other end of the teaching spectrum is encounter, when a learner is placed in an environment and actively tunes in. Here, learners get to know music by listening to it. In the brass-band world, they then have the opportunity to join in, playing an instrument with minimal instruction. In popular music learners encounter the music, then imitate the sounds. They often work for a long time, mastering one piece then starting over with another. Players accumulate the technical skills required to play particular pieces rather than, as in 'classical' music, studying pieces and engaging with technical exercises such as scales to improve mastery. Both methods work.

Sitting somewhere in the middle of instruction and encounter is teaching, characterized by the teacher encouraging different outcomes. Teaching dominates classroom work. It allows learners to follow their own ideas, learning by doing and experimenting. The skill of the teacher lies in knowing what to do next and in which direction to steer a learner. Teachers teach, facilitate and enable, creating opportunities to learn. These skills are encompassed in careful planning to ensure that all relevant material is covered and the needs of the individual learner are met.

INDIVIDUAL LESSONS

THE COMPONENTS OF A LESSON

A good instrumental lesson includes a variety of activities suited to the age and ability of the learner. There is more than one way of giving an effective lesson, and most teachers develop a routine that works for them. Many teachers begin with warm-up activities and go on to include some work with and without musical notation, including scales, aural development, studies and pieces. Whatever the mix of activities, there can be no doubt that the most effective lessons have practical music-making at the heart. Lessons in which teacher talk predominates are likely to be less successful, although there will always be occasions when lesson content, if taken in isolation, seems unbalanced.

Learning to read music

To be able to join an orchestra or band playing Western classical music, a learner needs to know how to read music, and so in lessons most teachers teach musical notation, and expect learners to develop fluency in reading. It is difficult to learn to read musical notation in the abstract, without the benefit of kinaesthetic learning: when holding an instrument, a child is more able to remember that pressing down a particular finger produces a given sound that correlates with a visual mark on a piece of music manuscript. The absence of kinaesthesia partly explains why singers are often less good at sight reading a new piece of music than orchestral and band players, who develop the skill to very high levels.

In certain genres, music is learnt by heart. For example, much pop music is performed without recourse to written notation, players usually learning the music aurally – by listening, imitating, and practising repeatedly until they've got it right. Few teachers work this way. The most effective teachers do, however, include some improvization – playing without written music – in lessons. Improvisation helps develop musical thinking skills and aural perception.

Lesson timing

Most private teachers give weekly 30-, 45- or 60-minute lessons. The length of a lesson increases as the learner gets older and more experienced. Lessons in schools range from weekly individual lessons of 15–20 minutes to group lessons lasting 25–35 minutes. For a beginner 20–30 minutes a week is adequate.

USING MUSIC TECHNOLOGY

For some teachers, music technology has become an essential part of their daily work. And for some instruments, music technology is an integral part of the playing itself, for example for electronic keyboards, drum kits and guitars. Even with a traditional instrument such as the violin, music technology can be used both to help the learner and support the teacher.

MIDI files

One of the driving forces in the development of musical technology was – and is – MIDI (Musical Instrument Digital Interface). Fortunately, when electronic keyboards were being developed in the early 1980s, manufacturers agreed to use a standard means of connecting together equipment from different sources , known as MIDI. By transferring sound digitally, it is possible to take sound and turn it into notation, hence the development of notation software that responds to signals from a MIDI keyboard. It is now possible for teacher, or pupil, to send a MIDI file by e-mail: the teacher might provide an accompaniment in the form of a backing track with which the pupil can practise.

THE TEACHER–PUPIL–PARENT RELATIONSHIP

Teacher and pupil is a two-way relationship that forms a partnership for learning. As with any partnership, it is important that both partners contribute to the relationship. The parental relationship can further complicate matters. Parents must be able to trust a teacher and let him manage both the learning process and the learner. From a teacher's perspective, there is nothing worse than a pushy parent who wants a child to be at the same stage as someone else's or pass an exam by a set deadline. Such parental pressure is unlikely to be in a learner's best interests. From a parent's point of view, there is nothing worse than a teacher who appears not to plan for the learning needs and progression of the child. From a child's perspective there's probably nothing worse than having a teacher in disagreement with a parent.

Some teachers like to involve parents in the learning process from the outset. With a younger child this can be very helpful: the parent not only ensures that regular practice is completed, but that the practice focuses on what the teacher wants the child to do. Other teachers prefer to develop a working relationship with the child that, on the face of it, almost excludes parents; this can work equally well. In an ideal world, all three participants jointly and severally manage the relationship. In the vast majority of cases, learning proceeds smoothly. On occasions when difficulties occur, the best advice is to talk with both teacher and child about a perceived problem as soon as possible, but before doing so, make sure there really is a problem, not just the perception of a problem.

GROUP LESSONS

A SOCIABLE ALTERNATIVE

Some teachers specialize in group teaching; others concentrate on providing one-to-one tuition. There is no right and wrong way of teaching someone to play a musical instrument. Most instruments can be taught in a group, and many children feel more comfortable and secure learning this way in the early stages.

Convincing evidence

Until recently, making the choice between individual and group lessons would have been a 'no-brainer': if you could afford it and wanted to make progress you booked individual lessons. Many teachers still subscribe to this point of view. But a great many more now recommend group lessons, particularly for beginners. There are many reasons for this change of thinking. First, children are used to learning in groups at school, particularly in primary schools. Second, peer group learning has been shown to be effective in music. Group instrumental learning makes ensemble music-making possible from the outset. Teaching groups is often more cost effective to deliver as well as cheaper for parents, and avoids problems in a society in which one-to-one work with children has become less acceptable.

That said, you may be offered the choice between group and individual lessons for practical reasons. As a parent, look at whether all options have been considered, or whether the teaching context is ruled by the attitude of the teacher rather than by the most effective teaching strategy.

Peer pressure

Sometimes children express an interest in learning an instrument because friends are learning the same instrument. If children are only taking part because friends are, however, think about whether this is appropriate and responsible. Another child might benefit from that scarce teaching place. Peer-group pressure can be beneficial in helping children persevere when the going gets tough, and socially it can help forge friendship groups. Older children can provide excellent role models in musical ensembles, and a group might enjoy playing and rehearsing outside lessons, perhaps busking as part of an informal entertainment at a school event.

The negative side of peer pressure arises when children are verbally abused for playing, or even carrying to school, a particular instrument. Report this type of bullying to the school, which should set anti-bullying strategies in action. Meanwhile, take action to ensure a child can continue with lessons and practise without feeling humiliated or embarrassed. At home, combat pressure brought about by siblings with encouragement and positive reinforcement to motivate and stimulate a child's interest.

SCHOOL OR HOME?

LESSONS AT SCHOOL

Instrumental lessons at school may be organized by a music coordinator or headteacher, or by the head of a music department. Instrumental teachers can be appointed by the school or provided by a local music service or independent agency. Whoever employs the teachers, when teaching takes place within a school, the school is responsible for the management and delivery of the tuition. Parents and children are unlikely to have much say in the teacher or space used, but can be reassured that safeguards are in place to ensure that both the classroom and teacher's conduct are appropriate.

How it works

Most schools charge for instrumental tuition. The school or agency providing tuition sets up a contract with parents indicating the number and duration of lessons per term or year, and stating whether they are taught one-to-one or as a group. Parental obligations – providing music books, instrument maintenance and so on – should be set out clearly at the contract stage, as should the process of ending the agreement if parent or child wish to discontinue tuition. You may wish to establish if the tuition leads to public examinations.

Some schools operate a selection policy if tuition places are limited. While this can be a pragmatic option, it can operate unfairly if selection involves a musical aptitude test. You might suggest to the organizing teacher that children who find the test difficult are likely to be most in need of tuition.

How to stay involved

When children have instrumental lessons at school, it's easy for parents to become isolated from the process. Take steps wherever possible to prevent such a situation developing. Many instrumental teachers expect children to bring a notebook to weekly lessons and use it as a simple way of communicating with parents, in much the same way as a school homework diary. Getting to meet a school's visiting instrumental teacher may be difficult. Ask if the teacher attends parents' evenings, make contact at a school concert, or simply send a note with a child asking for a meeting. You may also wish to speak to the person in the school who is the driving force behind instrumental learning – maybe the music coordinator or director of music. It can be useful to ascertain his or her commitment to musical activity at the outset of your child's learning.

Out-of-school classes

As well as providing school tuition, many music services run evening or Saturday morning centres that offer children the opportunity to join ensembles of an appropriate level for their ability and experience. Such ensembles or choirs are an invaluable addition to school instrumental lessons: playing in an ensemble helps motivate learners, improves standards and enhances awareness of musical matters. When making a decision about which instrument to begin playing, drop in at an evening or Saturday morning centre so a child can see her peers playing a broad range of instruments and styles of music. Ask also about demonstration sessions where she might be able to try out a range of instruments. For the very young you might find Kindermusik classes for babies, toddlers and their parents. Activities include singing, movement, making sounds with different instruments and listening.

My child is having lessons at school. Would he learn more quickly if I arranged additional private lessons?

Few, if any, teachers find it easy to pass on skills to a child if someone else is trying to teach those same skills at the same time. All teachers develop their own curricula and wish, quite properly, to emphasize different matters at different times. Learners become confused and irritated when being asked to prepare work for two people and, if they are conscientious about practising, are likely to become quickly overloaded.

LESSONS AT HOME

Teachers who offer instrumental or vocal tuition direct to parents and children are referred to as private teachers to distinguish them from teachers working directly for schools or music services. The vast majority of private music teachers are hard-working, enthusiastic musicians and teachers. Many give outstanding service for modest fees, often going the extra mile when additional preparation is needed for a musical event, such as a concert, exam or festival. Some teachers specialize in beginners and may use their more able students to assist them; others prefer to work with more experienced pupils and may arrange concerts and performances.

Choosing a private teacher

There is no easy way to choose a private music teacher, and in most parts of the world private instrumental teaching is not regulated by government or local authority. However, many teachers belong to a professional body (see pages 120–22) that exercises influence over its membership, and wherever possible ensures members have appropriate qualifications before admitting them as teachers. Other instrument-specific organizations may offer help and advice on finding a teacher (see pages 120–22).

You may be guided in your choice of teacher by your child's predilection for someone who is younger or older, male or female. Some teachers work well with young beginners and are able to continue with them through adolescence to maturity as individuals and musicians, while others are only highly effective with certain age groups or ability levels. Consider also levels of experience. The inexperience of a younger teacher may be counterbalanced by enthusiasm, or you may feel a slightly older, more experienced teacher would be right for your child's needs.

Many teachers offer a consultative or trial lesson, so before engaging a private teacher, do take this opportunity and stay with your child during the lesson. Check that the room is appropriate in size and layout, and that the equipment is suitable; this might include a piano, music stand, computer, CD player and speakers or computer software. This gives an indication – but no more – of a teacher's approach to work. The size of the room also allows you to judge whether a teacher needs to sit or stand very close to pupils. You might like to check the rapport between the teacher and the child.

Lessons in the home

Some private teachers are willing to teach at a pupil's home. This isn't an ideal option, since parents are then responsible for providing a space which is quiet, interruption-free and conducive to learning. The teacher may not have access to all the music he needs, nor to other essentials, such as a piano, CD player or computer.

Questions to ask

Before engaging a teacher, ask how many pupils he has and whether there is a waiting list. Ask how long the teacher has been teaching and how much time he spends teaching privately. Also enquire whether the teacher follows a curriculum and keeps up-to-date in teaching and learning skills by participating in professional development courses. You might like to find out whether he enters pupils for exams, festivals or competitions. Talking to parents of other pupils is likely to be informative, as is going to a concert at which the teacher's pupils are playing. It is always interesting to ask if a private teacher is active as a performing musician – something you might reasonably expect – or whether he or she has strong and valid reasons for no longer performing in public. Bear in mind that highly inspirational performers do not always make the best teachers. Ask if the teacher has been screened by police or a national criminal records bureau. Teachers who also work in schools have been checked. Others may have been screened as members of a professional association. If lessons take place at a teacher's home, check that you and your child feel comfortable with the room in which teaching takes place and ask about the teacher's experience with children.

How do I find a good teacher?

If your child starts lessons at school, it is unlikely that you will have a choice of teacher. To find a private teacher for home study, personal recommendation is always a good starting point: when you know a parent and child you are better able to judge whether the child has similar characteristics to your own. Look at the websites of musician' and teachers' organizations (see pages 120–22), which may maintain a register of teachers. Bear in mind that these lists are not comprehensive.

PRACTICE & PROGRESS

THE IMPORTANCE OF PRACTICE

There are no short cuts in the process of learning to play a musical instrument. The difference between success and failure depends on many factors, one of which is practice. To make progress when learning any instrument, practice is essential. Many adults look back on their experiences of learning to play and remember, with dread, being made to practise. Learning to enjoy practice time depends on effective teaching, a well-motivated learner and a supportive home situation. Expect to set aside a suitable time each day and a suitable place for this important homework to be done. With young children it's especially important to be involved from the outset: some teachers encourage parents to supervise practice, reminding the child of what the teacher said about a specific movement or sound.

How often to practise

The old adage of little and often is apposite – although parents of a child with a new drum kit or descant recorder may feel differently. Little and often is especially good for beginners because repetition of physical actions enables kinaesthetic learning to take place naturally. If a session isn't going well, it's best to stop and come back to it later: the frustration of not being able to do something hinders progress. As with most things, children benefit from a regular routine for practice. For the beginner, ten minutes of focused work every day is highly beneficial. Younger children who are up and about early in the morning may find practising before school is the best time to get it done, and this routine allows for additional playing after school, too, if desired. If this routine can be established, it should be easy to extend it to 20 or 30 minutes each day.

Where to practise

Before choosing an instrument it is important to plan where it will be stored and where and when practised. Many children like to practise in their bedroom. For best results make sure they have space to stand or that they sit on an appropriate chair rather than on the bed. If the child uses musical notation, acquire a music stand to develop good playing posture. The child might also need a CD or DVD player and speakers.

Supporting practice

Some teachers encourage children to use a range of technology to support learning, such as listening to musical examples on CD, DVD or video. A wide range of software has been designed to help learners, including programmes to help develop aural skills and the theory of music, which extends from understanding simple musical notation to more complex harmony and composition. Many teachers use MIDI (Musical Instrument Digital Interface) files to provide an accompaniment or backing to a piece of music. MIDI files can be played at differing speeds while maintaining pitch, or the pitch can be varied to match the player's choice of tempo. Recently developed software can 'follow' the player, allowing her to slow down for more difficult passages.

MAKING PROGRESS

Some learners have a natural aptitude for music and quickly pick up an understanding of the various elements as they master a chosen instrument. Others seem capable of making rapid progress but tire quickly of learning and look for a new pastime. Learners with less apparent aptitude may need more time to assimilate skills. With the right sort of teacher they can prosper, but more slowly. Progress for some children may be slow in terms of outcome – playing the music fluently. For such children celebrate progress in the satisfaction and success of enjoying lessons and being keen to practise. When learning becomes a chore and enjoyment disappears, it is time to think again.

The learning curve

Learning and mastering skills is not a smooth curve for most people, and progress in learning a musical instrument is not linear. It doesn't move forward inexorably day by day. Sometimes learners plateau and sometimes they appear to get worse. Learning new skills requires time for assimilation and consolidation, not only of physical motor skills but of concepts such as harmony, phrasing, dynamics, tone, intonation and timbre. Plateauing should be expected and allowed for by both learner and teacher. Acquiring the skills essential to master any instrument involves time, dedication and hard work. There are few, if any, successful performers who haven't spent hours practising.

When progress falters

Most children realize where they are in the pecking order of achievement. Exam or festival success, or otherwise, can help by providing an objective appraisal of performance, but sometimes it is necessary for parent or teacher to explain to a learner that her long-term goal may be unattainable, and this should be done kindly and in good time.

PRACTICAL MATTERS

ASSESSING THE COST

Although the benefits far outweigh the burden of cost, enabling a child to embark on learning an instrument represents a significant financial commitment. Before taking the plunge, consider the costs listed below. Bear in mind that school instrumental lessons may be subsidized: the opportunity to learn as part of a group has

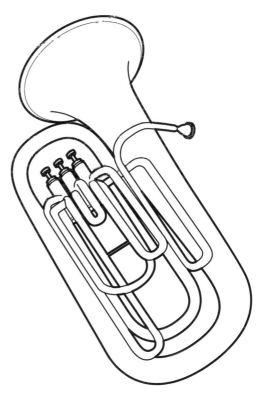

Likely costs
- paying for lessons
- hiring or buying an instrument
- acquiring a music stand
- sourcing music
- replacing reeds and strings
- buying accessories, such as mutes, tuner, metronome
- maintaining and tuning the instrument
- joining an ensemble
- attending a music centre
- entering competitions, festivals and exams
- dressing for concerts
- attending holiday courses
- touring with a group
- travelling to and from rehearsal
- taking time off work

financial benefits for parents as well as educational benefits for learners. Private teachers charge whatever fee they feel is appropriate (currently in the UK an average £20–40 per hour for most instruments). There is regional variation in fees and some teachers charge more if they know that there is a shortage of teachers for their instrument.

Ways to cut costs

You might like to organize a lift-sharing scheme to ease the burden and cost of ferrying children to and from rehearsals, or set up a fund-raising support group for children at Saturday or evening music centres. Meeting like-minded parents experiencing the same joys and difficulties with their own children's learning can be helpful. If you find the costs of learning difficult to accept, it may help to regard the outlay as a wise long-term investment. The child who is busy playing music spends fewer hours on computer games, has less time to do nothing, and is more likely to develop time-management skills in order to fit everything in. Players learn about music from the inside. This helps develop an understanding of creative processes and an ability to think creatively.

ACQUIRING AN INSTRUMENT

Before purchasing a new instrument, always try it out in the shop. There can be a world of difference between one model and another in terms of cost, sound and ease of sound production. Some instruments 'speak' more easily for no apparent reason. Never buy or rent an instrument without consulting the teacher. Some teachers have preferences for one make of instrument over another; some even refuse to teach on a particular make of instrument. Borrowing Uncle George's childhood clarinet is tricky: a teacher may be reluctant to tell child or parent that it is useless. As with other purchases, shop around for attractive discounts. There may be tax advantages in purchasing a new instrument through a school or local authority purchase scheme.

Buying second-hand

Choosing a second-hand instrument, like buying anything second-hand, is more risky than investing in a new instrument. If possible, take an expert with you when you go to buy, usually the instrumental teacher. What may seem like a bargain could be inappropriate or harder to play than an instrument designed for a beginner, need costly repair or be tuned to the wrong pitch. If a kindly relative promises to supply an instrument for a birthday, do have it vetted or selected by the child's teacher, or teacher-to-be. Buying an instrument at auction, either live or on-line, is risky unless you really know what you are doing and have either the teacher's backing or real-time support. On-line retail provides a simple and efficient way of purchasing music and accessories such as reeds and strings, but is only suitable for buying an instrument if the journey to the shop is impossible and the teacher has already been consulted.

Renting an instrument

Most instrument dealers operate rental schemes that offer some form of discount if, subsequently, you buy the instrument. This can be an ideal way to provide a child with the opportunity to learn on a good-quality instrument for a term or two before committing to an expensive purchase. Another advantage of the rental instrument is that it can be traded in or updated as necessary. Some schools and music services operate similar schemes.

Insuring your investment

Once the purchase or rental of an instrument is arranged, make sure to include it on an appropriate insurance policy. You regular household insurance may not cover the instrument when it travels by car, bus, train or foot to and from school. Find out whether your household insurance covers the instrument on school premises and check your car insurance, too. Some instrument cases are fitted with a lock and key. It may be best to put a spare key in a safe place.

BUYING MUSIC

Some teachers buy the music a pupil needs and then collect payment. Others are unwilling or unable to do this. While nothing beats browsing the shelves of a local music shop, many parents prefer to purchase music on-line, and this is an efficient way of dealing with the matter. Most experienced teachers are cost-conscious, and so neither expect pupils to purchase numerous new pieces of music, nor buy one expensive album and then only work on one piece.

Music and the law

Photocopying music is illegal in almost all circumstances, so it is unwise to accept photocopies from a teacher. By purchasing music you support music publishers, enabling the industry to survive financially and thus commission new works from composers and keep costs down. If you feel the music you are being asked to pay for is too expensive, ask the teacher if there is a more cost-effective choice. For exams there is almost always a choice of music. Exceptions are for instruments with a small repertoire of published music. The harp is a good example, where many pieces are very expensive. At the other extreme, there is a wide range of modestly priced music for clarinet and flute. Learners should be encouraged to develop their own collection of music. It can last a lifetime and may even be appropriate for their own children in the years to come.

Where to buy music

Good music retailers stock a broad range of music, including exam pieces and the syllabuses of various exam boards. These stores are a good source of birthday gifts, such as metronomes, electronic tuners, stationery and music cases. Staff get to know neighbourhood teachers, know what sells best and which pieces and albums of music the more effective teachers are purchasing. They are well placed to offer advice to parents, but music should rarely be purchased without seeking the teacher's advice. Teachers dread being confronted by a pupil with a piece of music bought for a birthday which is far too difficult for him to play.

KEEPING INSTRUMENTS CLEAN

Encourage children to wash their hands before playing any instrument. Pianos and keyboards show the evidence more than most. Good hygiene is especially important for woodwind and brass instruments. Discourage family members from having a blow and never share instruments with a mouthpiece or reed that touches the lips or inside the mouth. Teachers should lead by example. If an instrument has to pass from one player to another in lessons, make sure each player has his own reed or mouthpiece, or disinfect the mouthpiece. For brass instruments, recorders and flutes, this is straightforward, but the process is more difficult with reeds, since disinfectant may change the playing quality. Teachers will advise on how to keep the inside of the instrument clean, particularly important when coughs and colds are prevalent.

THE NOISE FACTOR

Some instruments generate a high volume of sound, particularly in the early stages of learning: the trumpet from the brass family and the oboe from the woodwind are good examples. Violins generate much less volume, but some parents find them equally difficult to tolerate! Before choosing an instrument, consider the impact of regular practice on other members of the household and on neighbours. Don't underestimate the effect on pets, either: dogs join in enthusiastically with instruments if the frequency of the sound

is in a particular part of their hearing range. An animal howling may be more irritating to a neighbour than the embryonic musical sounds being coaxed from an instrument.

Steps to take

To avoid excess disturbance for neighbours, locate upright pianos on a non-party wall if possible (and away from direct sunlight and central heating radiators). Modern uprights are fitted with practice pedals that can be locked into position, placing a felt bar against the strings to muffle the sound. This is good in many respects, but has the negative impact that a learner gets used to a sound which is not the true voice of a piano. Brass instruments can be fitted with a mute that allows them to be played almost silently, but for the same reason this is not ideal for an absolute beginner. Although a conventional drum kit generates a significant amount of noise, two substitutes may help. Practice pads – rubber discs used to help players acquire stick technique – reduce the sound dramatically, and electronic kits allow players to hear themselves on headphones with the rest of the household blissfully unaware.

Playing a musical instrument, unsurprisingly, involves noise at first, but it soon becomes a pleasant musical sound. Most beginners are unlikely to play for too long each day, so parents and families should simply prepare for this as part of the learning process. If it really does seem likely that this really will be too difficult to cope with, you might want to give serious thought as to whether a child should begin lessons at all.

THE WORLD OF MUSIC

EXAMS AND COMPETITIONS

Graded music examinations have been around for more than one hundred years. Several different independent exam boards offer examinations, and the format usually involves the preparation of pieces chosen from an exam syllabus, plus supporting tests, performed to an examiner, who awards marks and writes comments. After processing by the exam board, the results are forwarded to the teacher and then to the pupil and parents. A certificate is issued to successful candidates and a marksheet to all candidates.

The benefits of exams

Exams are highly motivational for many learners. They create the desire to outstrip peers and may help to induce daily practice. Most graded music exams can be taken by learners of any age, and although there are usually around eight grades, it is rarely a requirement of the exam board that all grades are taken. Used wisely by an effective teacher, they provide a milestone of achievement for pupils and a measurement of achievement to date.

Exams create a problem, however, when teachers respond to an exam syllabus by adopting it as a ready-made curriculum. Teaching to the test can result in poorly motivated pupils who may be good at passing exams but are not motivated to ucceed as musicians.

Competing in public

Competitions and festivals can be as motivating, or de-motivating, for learners as exams. The key difference is that the exam is essentially a private matter between candidate and examiner, whereas a competition or festival usually takes place in public, and the adjudication may be given verbally in public, followed by the distribution of written comments to participants and the celebratory award of a trophy. Some children find this a discouraging and even humiliating experience; you might like to join the audience as a family before submitting an entry form for such a competition.

Going on tour

Children who are regular members of a band or orchestra are often invited to take part on a tour to a festival hosted by another city or even another country. Scotland's Edinburgh Festival is a destination for many youth orchestras each year. A number of tour operators specialize in such work, organizing the travel and accommodation, arranging concerts at appropriate venues, and in some instances helping to guarantee audiences. Such trips are exhausting yet great fun, and though usually more costly than other school trips, need not be prohibitively expensive. As with any school visit, assure yourself that plans are properly organized before signing up, and make sure you factor in budgetary considerations if a group tours regularly. You might plan a family visit to a concert before a child starts lessons on an instrument if it seems likely that he may develop an interest in orchestral playing, the orchestral repertoire and the prospect of touring.

A CAREER IN MUSIC?

Of the many thousands of children who begin to learn an instrument, very few move into the music profession as performers. In the world of 'classical' music there are two key reasons: the number of vacancies for professional musicians is tiny, and standards are very high. For every player auditioned and selected to play in an orchestra, there may be another 50 who are equally good and yet rejected. That said, some instruments attract fewer learners than others, and whereas there may only be two or three clarinettists employed in an orchestra, there will be many more violinists, violists, cellists and double bass players. In the world of popular music, success is as much to do with effective promotion and marketing as it is with pure musical ability. In short, there are no rules for guaranteed success.

Joining an orchestra

Children who are making very good progress with instrumental learning tend to join a local youth orchestra, and may wish to consider a national youth orchestras as an ultimate goal. Why not approach music conservatoires to see if they run Saturday junior departments that offer access to high quality musical experiences?

Lifelong learning

Of those children who learn instruments associated with Western classical music, many do not continue music-making after leaving school. This mirrors the school process, which narrows down the number of subjects toward qualifications at 16 and 18, and then through higher education towards eventual employment. Musicians who do continue, or resume playing a little later, find a rich seam of amateur and semi-professional music-making open to them. Musical skills and experiences acquired through learning an instrument at school can never be considered as time lost or wasted.

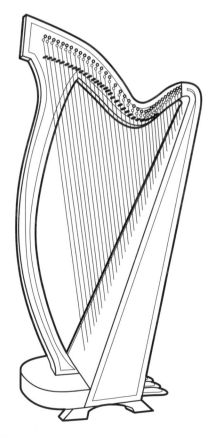

WHICH INSTRUMENT FOR MY CHILD?

THE PRACTICAL APPROACH

There are so many variables that it is impossible to give one simple answer to the question of which instrument your child should play. This book will help you to find out about most instruments available for a child to start playing, then weigh up the pros and cons of each instrument against the characteristics of your child in order to pick an instrument most likely to offer long-term success. However, there can be no guarantees that the chosen instrument is the right one. All too easily the decision can become the parent's rather than the child's.

In using this practical approach to choosing an instrument parents should bear in mind that many children will not carry on learning or reach the highest levels of achievement. Most children find it difficult to make a real choice about which instrument to start on. This can lead to false starts and perhaps greater parental expenditure, but the child gains invaluable experience on the way and a better chance of finding the right instrument in the end. There is a fine balance between the journey and the destination. Ask yourself which is more important.

There is no substitute for allowing music itself to influence the decision. Expose your children to as a wide a range of music as possible to help them form judgements about what appeals to them. The gut reaction to hearing a musical ensemble playing live could be the catalyst that makes your child say: 'I want to play one of those'. Urge your child to start taking part in music through singing, which provides an ideal starting point for many (although not all) children). Playing an instrument like the recorder, ocarina or some of the percussion family provides another easy-access route to ensemble music-making.

MAKING A CHOICE

Here are some pointers for ways in which to use this book to help you make a good choice of instrument to suit your learner. Read through the answers to each question below. When an instrument stands out as appropriate for your child's age, musical likes and personality or your home situation, jot it down on a piece of paper. It doesn't matter if more than one instrument seems suitable. You will find that some instruments suit more than one personality or learning style. Read about the options by turning to the pages that describe each instrument (pages 38-113). If the name of one instrument keeps jumping out, it could be the right one for your child.

1 Who wants to learn?

When starting to make a decision, think about who actually wants to learn the instrument: you or your child? Talk to your child to find out which instruments she might like to try. If she or you know already, making a choice is easy. Children with conviction – who know exactly which instrument they want to play – are usually right. Simply turn to pages 38–113 and read up about each one to see if it confirms your choice in terms of cost and practicalities as well as repertoire and ease of playing. If she doesn't know what she would like to try, move to question 2.

2 Which sounds does the learner prefer?

In order to identify the sounds of instruments and different styles of music, take time to listen to recordings and attend live performances together. Find ways to introduce live music into family life. Look for neighbourhood events, such as carnivals, festivals, concerts and religious occasions. Find out if local schools or music centres offer try-out sessions. Look for conservatoires that offer free concerts and Saturday morning workshops. Resurrect your neglected musical skills or encourage musicians in the family to share their knowledge and performance skills. Simply singing as a family on car journeys is a great start.

Which musical family? When you attend concerts or listen to CDs, try to pick out the sounds of the different musical families, asking your child whether he prefers the tone of strings or brass, woodwind, keyboards or percussion instruments. Read up on the musical families a child seems drawn to. Is he attracted within one family to a particularly sonorous instrument, such as the cello or harp, mandolin or oboe? Investigate that one further. Do allow older children in particular the chance to hear less common options, such as the tuba or French horn, double bass or harpsichord.

Which genre? Does your child prefer Western or Indian classical music, pop or rock, jazz or folk music, musicals or marching bands? Children who prefer jazz to classical pieces might be best steered toward instruments found in jazz ensembles, such as bass, drums, saxophone or trumpet. Those who enjoy string or wind groups to the instruments played in these ensembles. Investigate the instruments that reflect your family's heritage or the folk traditions of your region or neighbourhood if they attrac your child's ear.

How loud? Does music appeal if it is high or low in pitch, loud or quiet in dynamics? Children who like making noise might enjoy the drum kit or a brass instrument. Listeners find the tone of some instruments instantly turns them on or off, which narrows options well. Tactile children might like the cello, which rests against the body during playing for total immersion in sound.

3 How old is the learner?

Some instruments are good to start learning young. Others require prior skills on a similar instrument, a larger physique or hand span, or more developed facial muscles. Read up on the choices below that suit specific age groups to see if they match your child's choice in music and preference for dynamics. Can the child carry the instrument in its case into school and back (or even across the playground) without your help? Use your discretion if a child is small or large for his age, and take advice from an experienced music teacher. If your child has started on one instrument and would like to try or move to another, also take advice from his teacher.

5–8 years? From the preschool years, nurseries and parent and toddler groups expose children to a range of percussion instruments. From five years these are good places to start learning music. Why not look at the djembe drum in more detail? The recorder and ocarina suit this age group – ocarina is an ideal starter instrument for younger children. Manual dexterity is important on piano and violin, and many children do well starting young while digits are malleable. Some

instruments are naturally small, such as the cornet. Others are made in a variety of sizes to accommodate learners with small hands: look at the violin, viola and cello. If the sound of the double bass appeals, read up on how mini-basses enable children as young as six to begin learning. If your child is attracted to the clarinet, look at the sized-down Kinder-Klari and Lyons C clarinets that also suit children from six years on. Mini trombones make an easy-to-sound instrument available to this younger age group.

8 years upwards? Some instruments come into their own for children aged eight or nine, or who are moving towards the final years of primary school. The flute is a good example, although models with curved headjoints allow younger children to start if they don't want to learn fife, recorder or ocarina first. Suitable instruments for this age group also include the guitar, clarinet and relatively cumbersome and tricky to pitch French horn. Sized-down instruments are still appropriate in this age bracket: the mini bassoon offers a way into this large instrument. Other children will be ready to move on from a starter instrument. Those who have spent a couple of years learning clarinet might try the saxophone; those who began the cornet, the trumpet.

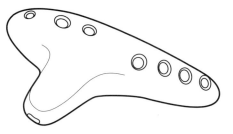

A child's handspan helps determines which of the bowed string instruments might be the best starting point for string-playing. As does an increased ability to care for or carry an instrument, for instance the neck of a bass guitar can be difficult for younger children to handle.

10 years upwards Instruments best suited to older children – aged 11–12 and up – include all those which were previously too bulky or heavy to handle or carry to and from school and rehearsal. Now is the time to look at instruments on which it can be more difficult to make a sound, such as oboe, or that require a larger sized hand, such as bassoon. A child who has mastered the basics on one instrument may like to graduate to a larger, heavier or full-size instrument within the family, moving perhaps from cornet or trumpet to euphonium or tuba, French, tenor or baritone horn. String players may transfer from violin to viola. As children's voices become deeper it may become easier to tackle lower pitched instruments, such as cello, double bass, tuba, trombone, euphonium.

4 What about the child's aptitudes and learning style?

How a child works in school lessons and the way she prefers to learn can help dictate which types of instruments she might be drawn to. Other issues of personality and temperament should also be taken into account.

Does your child like reading?

Children who find reading easy may do well with an instrument that requires a player to read music; this includes most of the 'classical' instruments of the orchestra. Those who dislike reading might do better with instruments taught more through aural exploration: instruments used in traditional music and brass bands, and keyboards, bass and drums as used in pop and rock music. Having good aural perception – being able to hear a note before playing it – makes learning unfretted strings, such as violin, viola and cello, less frustrating, and can help novice brass players recognize intonation problems.

How about coordination skills?

Instruments in which both hands (and even both feet) carry out independent tasks simultaneously, and that also require a player to read differing lines of music, may be more suited to those with good coordination. These include piano, electronic keyboards and especially the pipe organ. Orchestral stringed instruments and drum kit also call for multi-tasking. An instrument that plays a single line, from recorder to bass guitar, may prove easier to master.

Will your child practice and persevere? Perseverance can make success more likely on some instruments: those on which it is initially difficult to sound a note, such as flute and even more so oboe, which demands control and mastery to develop a good sound and tone. Perseverance helps also with instruments on which the player has to pitch notes, such as violin, viola and French horn, probably the easiest brass instrument of all to mispitch. These instruments require a child who is patient and serious about learning. Bowed strings

generally suit a 'serious' child, though cello and double bass are easier to learn since players can watch what they are doing and pitch accuracy is less of an issue. Some instruments are relatively simple to start, but require commitment and, above all, practice if a learner is to develop fluency (piano), intonation (clarinet) or 'keep in' the lip (the brass family). Percussion suits learners with a clear sense of purpose, since the percussion player is responsible for keeping a group in time.

Other instruments may suit children who require more instant gratification to remain motivated: it's easy to play a note on a piano and pick out a tune, to run up and down the notes of a saxophone, or make a sound on a trombone, tenor or baritone horn. On some instruments mistakes are less obvious: double bass is an example. All might suit children who are easily discouraged.

Solitary nature or group player?

Does your child prefer learning in a group to solitary study? If so, she might like the companionship of group violin, guitar or recorder lessons, brass-band style learning, or to take up percussion in a samba band or with the djembe drum. Or she may enjoy an instrument popular with her peers, such as guitar or flute. Children who work well in a team might choose instruments played in the orchestra or which make up smaller wind or string ensembles. Those who like to feel part of a family would feel comfortable with the teaching style and camaraderie of a brass band (key instruments include cornet and tenor and baritone horns). Those who like to 'drive' a group may relish percus-

sion playing or drum kit, children who like to lead a group bass instruments, such as tuba, bassoon and double bass. For some children it's important to pick an instrument with a 'cool' image to impress their peers: you might consider the guitar, bass guitar, saxophone or djembe drum.

Children who prefer solitary pursuits may more easily adjust to instruments that are more often taught one-to-one, such as cello, French horn or piano. They also might like those with a wide solo repertoire, including violin, piano, electric keyboards or trumpet. Some instruments can even be self-taught: read up on the harmonica, banjo or even bass guitar.

Outgoing or quiet? Very confident children may enjoy learning an instrument that turns heads when they start to play, such as the trumpet (its tone does not suit the timid) or more 'showy' instruments, like the euphonium. Some children thrive on public performance. Steer them towards the instruments of the brass or marching pipe bands, to samba and steel pan groups or instruments welcome in amateur operatic performances. Can-do personalities and children with plenty of energy tend to get on with the brass family. Those who have the confidence to come in at the right time on a loud instrument might relish the larger orchestral percussion instruments.

Children who prefer a behind-the-scenes role might play viola to the extrovert's violin (viola plays a more supportive role in ensemble playing) or the French horn, an instrument that helps strings and woodwind instruments meld together well. Those who wish to be sought-after as ensemble musicians could learn the oboe, bassoon, bass guitar, French horn or tuba: players of these instruments are always in demand and the playing opportunities they offer bring a welcome boost of self-esteem.

How careful is your child? Some instruments require a child with the disposition to look after sensitive parts, for example, to adjust strings and reeds and keep elements dry and clean. These include strings and wooden woodwind instruments, and trombones, whose slides must be protected from damage and dents. Some instruments, such as the clarinet, must be assembled before every playing session, which might not suit less careful or agile-fingered children.

5 Practical considerations

Cost, space (in the home, car and head) and time demands all have a bearing on which instrument best suits your household and family routine. Go back over all the choices you have earmarked so far and assess how they meet these very practical criteria.

Can you afford the instrument? Pages 38–113 set out the likely cost of each instrument new and second-hand. Some beginners' instruments are priced very modestly: the acoustic guitar, fiddle, violin and viola, trumpet and cornet. The mouth organ is eminently affordable, and cheapest of all are the ocarina and recorder. The latter may even be provided free at school. There is a thriving second-hand market for other instruments, including electric guitar, flute, saxophone, tenor horn and piano. Some instruments are more expensive because they are less common options. These includes bass guitar, French horn, cello, baritone horn, euphonium and tuba. If cost is of no consequence, you might consider the most expensive options, too: orchestral harp, grand piano, sitar or Great Highland pipes. Remember to take into account not only the cost of the instrument, but of essential accessories, such as an amplifier and leads, music stand and carrying or travel cases. Consider also running costs by looking at the individual page entries. Some instruments require only cheap replacement strings or reeds, others expensive professional tuning. The orchestral harp even has expensive music. Finally, consider the price of lessons. Some may be free, such as the process of sitting in with a brass band or folk group, and can be a good place to get a feel for playing and instrument options. Lessons at school, especially in groups, are cheaper than those that require a private teacher.

Are teachers and instruments available? In most towns there will be a ready supply of private teachers and school lessons in the traditional instruments learned by beginners. However, choice may be restricted by the group lessons on offer at school. For teachers of more unusual or traditional instruments you may have to venture further afield. Teachers of folk and non-Western instruments tend to be found more easily only in certain geographical regions. For instruments such as the concertina you may even have to attend specialist summer camps.

Ask whether your child's school has a ready supply of instruments – it may even hand out recorders, ocarinas and classroom percussion instruments. For other choices you may have to seek out specialist sellers by taking a teacher's advice or even through a web search.

Can you store and transport it?

Is your car large enough to transport a drum kit or double bass, euphonium or tuba? If not, does a pocket-sized ocarina or mouth-organ suit your circumstances better right now? Transport is not just an issue of fitting large items into the car, but of putting aside time to drive and wait for rehearsals to end. If you mind giving up your weekend and evenings to ferry children around, steer a child away from brass or pipe bands and the steel pans and toward a small instrument that's played at home.

Is there a quiet place at home for practice?

Make sure your choice of instrument can be accommodated in a bedroom or other quiet place for practice. If you lack space an instrument that plays silently once the child puts on headphones might be the answer, such as an electronic keyboard or drums. Alternatively, look at instruments that are only practised at school, such as the large orchestral percussion or steel pans, or large instruments that can only be brought home at weekends and holidays, such as double bass. You might even consider an instrument based elsewhere, such as a church pipe organ!

REFERENCE CHARTS

Each instrument in Part Two, Choosing an Instrument (pages 38–113) has a quick-reference chart, which provides information on the suitability of the instrument for a beginner, including the investment needed, availability, size and weight information and how easy it is to learn to play.

The greater the number of ♩, the better the instrument suits a beginner. Those marked with ♩♩♩♩♩, for example, will be relatively cheap to buy new, freely available second-hand, reasonable to maintain, light to carry and not too difficult to learn.

In the example opposite you can see that pianos are relatively expensive to buy new, but are widely available second hand. They are fairly expensive to maintain, are

heavy (though do not need to be carried around by the leaner, of course), are relatively difficult to learn to play and are available in smaller than standard versions.

The quick-reference information for every instrument is summarized in a chart on pages 114–115.

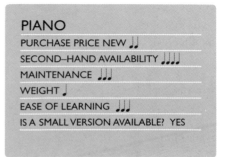

PIANO

PURCHASE PRICE NEW ♩♩
SECOND–HAND AVAILABILITY ♩♩♩♩
MAINTENANCE ♩♩♩
WEIGHT ♩
EASE OF LEARNING ♩♩♩
IS A SMALL VERSION AVAILABLE? YES

PART TWO

CHOOSING AN
INSTRUMENT

In this part of the book you will find detailed information about instruments commonly taught in schools or privately to beginners, grouped within their various families of instruments. In order to make an informed decision, as well as reading about the specific instrument in which you are interested, why not look at similar instruments in the family, and make comparisons with instruments from other families, too?

STRING FAMILY

Stringed instruments divide into two categories: those that are exclusively plucked and tend to have frets (metal strips across the fingerboard), and those that also make a sound when a bow is drawn across the strings. The harp is an exception; it has no bow, fingerboard nor frets and the strings are plucked.

Where to hear the instruments

In the symphony orchestra, strings work as part of a section that can include as many as 24 violins, divided into two parts (first and seconds), eight violas, twelve cellos and eight double basses. The violin, viola, cello and double bass all have four strings, tuned to G–D–A–E on the violin, C–G–D–A on the viola and cello, and E–A–D–G on the double bass. They share a body shape and design that has changed little since their development in the early 17th century. The instruments are made of wood held together with glue and the bow is wood with horsehair, or synthetic fibre.

Strings in popular and folk music

The most common of the plucked stringed instruments, the guitar can be heard in folk and popular music genres as well as in classical works. Its six strings tuned to E–A–D–G–B–E are plucked with the fingers or using a plectrum, a flexible plastic pick. The guitar's electric counterpart is played in a similar fashion to provide a chordal backing, lead melody or mixture of both. The bass guitar, with its four strings tuned E–A–D–G, provides a bass line.

The oldest member of the string family takes two forms today: the smaller folk harp or clarsach played in traditional music, and the orchestral harp. The clarsach is more portable and quieter in tone than the difficult-to-transport orchestral harp. The mandolin, ukulele and banjo are, like the sitar, less commonly taught in school.

What makes a string player?

String players often seem to be the more serious members of the orchestra. They have to look after their relatively fragile instruments, maintain the bow and deal with tuning. Playing a bowed stringed instrument requires sophisticated coordination, perseverance and good aural perception, or the ability to hear a note 'internally' before playing it. The absence of frets on a fingerboard means some string players have to learn where notes are, although guitarists are provided with an indication of where to place fingers. When first learning, children may experience some discomfort with sore fingers, which a good teacher will guard against while strength builds during the early stages of learning.

VIOLIN

VIOLIN

PURCHASE PRICE NEW ♪♪♪♪

SECOND–HAND AVAILABILITY ♪♪♪

MAINTENANCE ♪♪♪♪♪

WEIGHT ♪♪♪♪

EASE OF LEARNING ♪♪

IS A SMALL VERSION AVAILABLE? YES

Learning to play the violin takes a good deal of time, patience and perseverance, but an accomplished player gains access to some of the world's most beautifully written music, and many violinists go on playing and performing to a very advanced age.

Repertoire

The violin has the largest repertoire of all Western classical instruments, other than the piano. Most violinists play as part of a group, and music for the violin includes ensemble and orchestral compositions from the late Baroque period through the Classical and Romantic eras to the present day. The violin features as a solo instrument in the concertos of Tchaikovsky, Beethoven, Brahms, Mozart and many other composers. As part of a string quartet (comprising two violins, a viola and a cello), the violin can be heard in light and popular music of the mid and late 20th century. It is played in jazz ensembles, like the quintet of the Hot Club of France, and much music has been written for violin and piano.

How it is played

The instrument and classical technique remain largely unchanged since the violin's development in the late 16th century. Sounds are made by drawing a bow, usually held in the right hand, across the strings or, on some occasions, by plucking the strings with the right hand. Difficulty of bowing is exacerbated by the instrument's positioning, held beneath the left side of the chin, too close to be looked at comfortably and clearly.

Learning the violin

Beginners are often taught in small groups and sometimes in classes of up to 30 children. Learning as part of a group may help children develop aural skills more readily and maintain motivation. Teaching methods such as Suzuki focus on tone production, aural development and memorizing, with less emphasis on written notation and learning to read music. As with any instrument, quality of teaching is paramount, regardless of the method adopted. Ensemble activity is likely to motivate beginner violinists, and so opportunities to play with a group at school, or perhaps in the evening or at weekends, are important.

Aptitude and temperament

Violins are made in all sizes, so even very young children can learn to play, but success depends on good hand-eye coordination, plus patience and perseverance on the part of the player and, when within earshot, parents too! In the hands of a beginner, the violin makes a sound that many find less than attractive for some time. Playing the violin requires simultaneous independent activity with each hand, something some children find difficult.

Cost and maintenance

The purchase price for a first instrument is modest, but as quality increases, so does price – dramatically. There is a plentiful supply of second-hand instruments, although many parents prefer to buy a new one. Running costs for a violin are minimal. Expect to buy replacement strings, which can wear out, or break when stretched by over-enthusiastic tuning. Bows need to be re-haired from time to time, and the adjustment mechanism may require occasional maintenance. The violin is sensitive to rough handling and changes in temperature, so store away from direct sunlight or sources of heat.

Size and weight

The violin is available in three-quarter, half, quarter and even smaller scaled-down sizes (up to $\frac{1}{32}$ of the standard instrument), enabling even the smallest player to handle it. Most players start on a half- or quarter-size instrument and move on to full size as soon as they grow sufficiently. The instrument and bow are not heavy, and modern lightweight, waterproof cases have done away with the gangster's machine-gun image.

Violin and bow

VIOLA

The viola is commonly taught in schools as a beginner's instrument. Many adult violinists also play and teach viola. In much orchestral music, the viola plays an important but sometimes rather dull role, providing neither the glamour nor drama of the tune, nor the strength of a bass line. Perhaps it is for this reason that the instrument – and sometimes the player – has become the butt of musicians' jokes. However, the list of viola players in history is illustrious, including Mozart, Haydn and Beethoven.

Repertoire

The role of this instrument in the orchestra is a vital one, and so playing the viola almost certainly means playing in a symphony orchestra, string orchestra or string quartet. While there may be opportunities at school to play a broad range of music, in the longer term, a violist plays the repertoire associated with these ensembles. A number of fine works have been written for the viola, including concertos by two great English composers: Sir Malcolm Arnold and Sir William Walton.

How it is played

The viola is held, like the violin, beneath the left side of the chin and the player 'stops', or presses, the strings on to the fingerboard with her left hand to change the pitch of notes while making the sound either by plucking strings with the right hand or drawing a bow across them.

Learning the viola

It is possible to play music written for the viola on a violin strung and tuned as a viola. In a school with a number of children learning stringed instruments, the teacher may do this as a way of introducing children to the instrument, providing an intermediate step in the process of transferring from violin to viola. Some violins are specially adapted with a 'hole' drilled in the front, which produces a much better quality viola sound.

Aptitude and temperament

Music written to include the viola and the processes associated with learning are similar to the violin (see pages 42–43), for example good hand-eye coordination is important. However, since the viola plays from notation in a different clef – the viola or alto clef – players have to be able to learn another form of notation.

Cost and maintenance

The purchase price of a viola is modest and second-hand instruments are readily available. Many parents prefer to buy a new instrument, but do ask a teacher's advice. As with the violin, running costs are minimal: replacement strings are the main expense, along with occasional re-hairing of the bow.

Size and weight

Like the violin, violas are made in smaller sizes to accommodate smaller players, but learners who move to the viola from the violin are less likely to do so until they are playing on a full-size instrument. Although the instrument and bow are a little heavier than the violin, most children can manage to carry the viola to and from school and lessons.

Viola and bow

CELLO

CELLO
PURCHASE PRICE NEW ♩♩♩
SECOND–HAND AVAILABILITY ♩♩♩♩
MAINTENANCE ♩♩♩♩
WEIGHT ♩♩♩
EASE OF LEARNING ♩♩♩
IS A SMALL VERSION AVAILABLE? YES

The cello – its full name is violon-cello – is quite a fragile instrument and even smaller-sized versions are quite bulky to carry. It provides the lowest notes in a string quartet and produces a sound that many children find appealing. The instrument rests against the player, which allows players to feel as well as hear the notes.

Repertoire

As with the violin (see pages 42–43), playing the cello almost certainly means playing in a symphony orchestra, string orchestra or string quartet. This instrument's repertoire is huge, and principally lies in musical genres other than jazz and popular music. Music is written mostly in the bass clef, although players occasionally use the tenor clef.

How it is played

Since the instrument is played sitting down, the player can look and see what she is attempting to do and this makes learning easier than for the viola or violin. In common with these instruments, the left hand 'stops' the strings against the fingerboard while the right hand draws the bow over the strings.

Learning the cello

The same issues apply as with the violin and viola (see pages 44–45). Although not an easy instrument to play, cello learners tend to produce good results more quickly than novice violin players.

Aptitude and temperament

Coordination skills associated with playing the violin, such as the ability to use each hand independently, apply equally to the cello. For some beginners the cello can be difficult because it plays notes outside a child's vocal range. Only trying the instrument will reveal if it is likely to cause a problem. Those who like to be part of a team will be pleased to find that even a player with modest facility on the instrument is welcome in a school ensemble, which almost always lack instruments to play the lower bass notes of a piece. The principle applies as more progress is made, leading to playing opportunities in local amateur or youth orchestras.

Cost and maintenance

Beginners' instruments are more modestly priced than professional models, but as with the violin, the sky's the limit for a really good one. The purchase price is reasonable for a mid-range instrument and there is fairly ready second-hand supply. As with all instruments, follow a teacher's advice whether buying a new or second-hand model. Running costs are minimal, replacement strings and occasional maintenance the main items. However, cellos are easily damaged, particularly in the hurly-burly of school life, and repairs can be costly. Cases are essential and range from a canvas cover (almost historic) that affords minimal protection to lightweight hard cases that survive almost anything. Second-hand instruments may be sold without a case; beware of the additional cost of replacing it.

Size and weight

Like violins and violas, cellos are available in scaled-down versions to suit the size and handspan of a young beginner. The weight of the instrument is taken by a spike which rests on the floor. Full-size cellos weigh a good amount. They are bulky and not particularly easy to carry so younger children will require the help of an adult, and probably a car, to carry one to and from lessons. The bow is heavier than that of a violin or viola.

Cello and bow

DOUBLE BASS

The largest and lowest pitched member of the string family, the double bass has four strings. It is a versatile instrument and players can transfer easily to electric bass to access contemporary popular music. It is a relatively easy instrument on which to hear results quickly and so might be considered for beginners more often than it is.

Repertoire

The repertoire for double bass embraces the full range of orchestral and string music. Symphony orchestras may include as many as eight double basses, chamber orchestras perhaps just two, and smaller ensembles usually have one. Parts for this instrument are written for the symphonic wind band and, of course, it improvizes in jazz ensembles.

How it is played

The player stands, or sits on a high stool, and the instrument rests on a spike. The left hand 'stops' the strings against the fingerboard while the right hand draws the bow over the strings. There are two commonly used versions of the double bass bow, the French and the German, and each has a different hold and playing technique associated with it. In jazz ensembles the bass is usually played pizzicato, the strings plucked by the right hand.

Learning the double bass

The double bass is available in a mini-bass format for young beginners and so suits children aged 6–10 years and upwards. The instrument's size makes it musically forgiving and, although not easier to play to a very high standard than other string instruments, pitch inaccuracies and sound imperfections can be much less noticeable. The transition to bass guitar (see pages 54–55) is easy for most players, who often find that instrument less physically demanding than its classical counterpart.

Aptitude and temperament

This instrument attracts comparatively few learners, despite being in many respects easier than the violin, viola or cello, and so is a great instrument to choose as a beginner, especially for someone who enjoys a sense of getting somewhere quickly. For those who like to be sociable and enjoy performing, the double bass brings frequent opportunities to play, since players are welcome in many different ensembles. Players gain a real sense of leadership by providing the bass to an ensemble.

Cost and maintenance

The double bass is more expensive to buy than a violin, viola or cello. The purchase price is significant and although the second-hand market is quite good and a large number of instruments are in circulation, finding a good one can be difficult. Running costs are minimal, although replacing strings, which fortunately does not happen too often, can be costly.

Size and weight

A full-size double bass is one of the most heavy and cumbersome instruments detailed in this book. It is not easily transported without adult assistance, which may confine home practice sessions for the younger beginner to weekends and holidays. The double bass comes in smaller sizes, however, and most adult players actually use a three-quarter size instrument. Popular since the 1980s, a mini-bass size has encouraged children as young as six to take up the instrument, since transporting it to and from school for lessons is not too difficult.

Double bass

HARP

The orchestral harp is a large, heavy, mechanically complex and expensive instrument, whether acquired second-hand or new. Its range is similar to that of a piano, with the player using a system of pedals to change notes produced by plucking the 46 strings, which are fewer in number than those of a piano. The harp's ability to add colour and mood to a piece has made it an essential part of a composer's palette. For information about smaller harps used in traditional music, see page 113.

Repertoire

The harp came to prominence in the orchestrations of Romantic and 20th-century composers, and so many pieces written for the instrument date from these periods.

How it is played

The player sits with the instrument in front of him, plucking the strings using both hands, one on each side of the instrument. All fingers except the little ones are used in plucking.

Learning the harp

Harp teachers are quite scarce, and lessons are unlikely to be readily available at school. Most children begin learning on a small harp which avoids many transportation problems and makes the financial outlay more bearable.

Aptitude and temperament

Children are rarely exposed to the harp; if they are, they are likely to know for certain whether they wish to learn it. In this respect the instrument chooses the learner. Learning to play the harp is a bigger commitment for learner and parents than many other instruments, so give plenty of time and thought to the decision-making process. Children beginning lessons may experience some discomfort, such as sore fingers. A good teacher will guard against excessive discomfort while strength builds up during the early stages of learning. The size of the child and his handspan may be another factor to bear in mind: any harp teacher should be more than willing to give you advice if you have any doubts or questions.

Cost and maintenance

An orchestral pedal harp is expensive – it costs probably as much as the car required to transport it. There are a limited number of knowledgeable second-hand dealers. Maintenance, mechanical repairs and replacement strings are costly, and additional expenditure comes In the form of a cover and trolley for moving. The orchestral harp is an instrument to be considered very carefully if your child expresses an interest in it.

Size and weight

Harps near 2 m (6 ft 8 in) in height and weigh a hefty 35 k (77 lb). They require a car for transportation. If a child has lessons at school, the instrument may only be able to be moved home for practise at weekends and holidays.

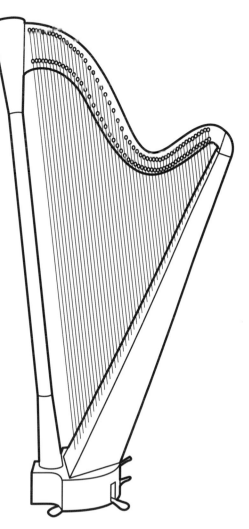

Concert harp

ACOUSTIC GUITAR

Acoustic, like electric, guitars are popular, versatile and often inexpensive instruments, and one of the few easily portable musical instruments that can provide a chordal accompaniment for a singer. An acoustic guitar has six strings, and the fingerboard on most models features frets – metal strips laid crossways to help a player see and feel where the fingers go. An acoustic guitar is a gentle instrument.

Acoustic guitar

Repertoire

The acoustic guitar can be used to accompany a singer or to play a wide range of classical compositions. It features in jazz improvisation and folk genres.

How it is played

A classical guitar rests on the player's lap and she places one foot on a footstool. For other styles of music, acoustic guitars are held by a neck strap and the strings are plucked or strummed ('licked') by a plectrum; the other hand depresses them on the fretboard to create notes or chords.

Learning the guitar

The guitar is often taught in large groups. Some players learn to read from notation, others from chords. Children learning the guitar may learn chord shapes: memorizing three or four allows a player to accompany many popular songs.

Aptitude and temperament

Playing requires high levels of coordination, and music written for classical guitar can look and be difficult to read.

Cost and maintenance

There is a ready second-hand market for acoustic guitars. Prices can be modest for a new beginner's instrument. They are relatively fragile so you might consider a sturdy carrying case. Add the cost of replacement strings.

Size and weight

Guitars are neither heavy nor cumbersome.

ELECTRIC GUITAR

Electric guitars, like the acoustic instruments, are popular, versatile and often inexpensive instruments, and one of the few easily portable musical instruments that can provide a chordal accompaniment for a singer. They have six strings and the fingerboard on most models features frets – metal strips laid crossways to help a player see and feel where the fingers go. Electric guitars require an amplifier – bear in mind noise levels if you plan to host band rehearsals.

Electric guitar

Repertoire

Electric guitarists, often playing in pop groups, usually memorize music, but those who learn to read from notation or chord symbols gain access to a broader repertoire.

How it is played

Electric guitars are usually held with a strap, and strings, which are made from steel, are strummed with a plectrum. They plug into an amplifier with a lead.

Learning the guitar

The guitar is often taught in large groups. Some players learn to read from notation, others from chords. Children may learn chord shapes: memorizing three or four allows a player to accompany many popular songs, and creating a rhythmic feel by strumming these chords in different ways is good first step to improvisation.

Aptitude and temperament

Playing requires high levels of coordination and it can be beneficial to start on the acoustic guitar.

Cost and maintenance

There is a ready second-hand market for electric guitars but if possible have a teacher or guitar professional check a second-hand guitar is up to scratch before purchasing. Consider the extra expense of an amplifier and add the cost of replacement strings and electronic tuning devices.

Size and weight

Electric guitars come in different sizes.

BASS GUITAR

The bass guitar is tuned to the same notes as the double bass (see pages 48–49), being an electric version of that instrument. It is electronically amplified like the electric guitar. The instrument was developed in the 1920s and mass production began in the 1950s. Since then, the instrument has become a core component of pop and rock music. Bass players are much sought after, particularly those who can work from notation as well as play by ear.

Repertoire

The instrument can provide a bass part in any form of popular music ensemble, combo or band, as well as in jazz improvisation. It is rarely, if ever, played as a solo instrument, and consequently relies on ensemble music-making. Like all instruments, sheet music is widely available: ask a teacher to direct you to a good retailer.

How it is played

The instrument is held by a neck strap and plugged into an amplifier with a lead. The strings are plucked or strummed, often with a plectrum, a flexible plastic pick, in the right hand. The left hand depresses the strings on the fingerboard to create notes. The instrument has slightly fewer capabilities than a regular guitar.

Learning bass guitar

A single note instrument that rarely plays chords, the bass, with its four strings, is often considered to be easier to learn than the six-string guitar, although it requires coordination of both hands. Most players find the instrument less physically demanding than its classical counterpart. Children may be keen to learn the bass (and guitar) without input from a teacher. This is certainly possible and to an extent is true of all instruments. However, some teacher input makes learning much more straightforward and, in most cases, more effective.

Aptitude and temperament

Bass guitar may be an ideal second instrument for children who already learn an instrument that does not lend itself to ensemble music-making. The bass shares the cool credibility of the electric guitar, which may attract some players, and tends to be a good choice for those who enjoy improvising and youngsters keen to become part of a team or 'scene' but avoid the limelight. Players gain a real sense of leadership by providing the bass to an ensemble.

Cost and maintenance

Many second-hand instruments are available, but both the musical and electrical qualities of the instrument need to be tested before purchase. New instruments are modestly priced, but do ascertain the quality and accuracy of the fingerboard and frets before buying. Build in the initial expense of buying an amplifier.

Size and weight

The instrument is made in a variety of shapes and sizes, though scaled-down versions for young beginners are not available. Although not particularly heavy, the instrument can be cumbersome to carry around because of its long neck. It is easier to move than a double bass, although the amplifier adds to difficulties with transportation.

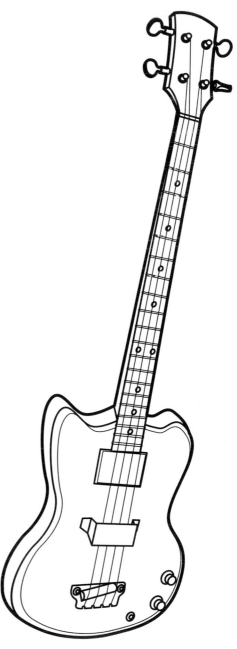

Bass guitar

SITAR

Considered to be the most popular Indian classical musical instrument, the sitar has become more widely known in the West since the 1960s. It is a melodic rather than a chordal instrument and its Western equivalent is the lute (see pages 58–59). The neck and sound board are made of wood and the gourd is a hollowed and dried pumpkin. The size of the gourd regulates the sound the instrument produces.

Repertoire

The traditional music played on the sitar is Indian classical music. It is improvised and heartfelt. The emotional quality is provided not just by the sequence of notes played but also by the small inflections, or changes in pitch, given to each note.

How it is played

The sitar has up to 20 strings, of which up to six or seven are used to play, with four typically active. The remaining strings are referred to as sympathetic because they vibrate in sympathy with those struck by the player. Some of the sympathetic strings function as drones, sustained bass notes. The active strings are plucked with a metallic plectrum, or *mezrab*, worn on the index finger. A player sits on the floor.

Learning the sitar

The sitar is a difficult instrument to tune and play, and learning to play it well is a lifelong project and cultural experience. Notes are far apart, so the hands move up and down a lot, and the action is high, requiring strong fingers to press down on the strings. Frets are curved and moveable as well as raised, and hitting the correct fret is difficult. Traditionally, learners are apprenticed to a master, but this is a less common teaching method outside the Indian subcontinent. The bass version of the sitar is called a Surbahar and has a wider and longer neck with fixed frets.

Aptitude and temperament

The instrument may have most appeal to children from a cultural background matching the origin of the instrument, since learning to play sitar involves learning to understand Indian classical music. Both learner and parent need to be aware of this from the outset.

Cost and maintenance

Even a beginner's sitar is relatively expensive and, as with most instruments, price increases with quality. Look for a specialist retailer or consult a teacher before buying online and make sure an expert checks the frets. Running costs are high because replacement strings are not cheap. Sitars require regular cleaning and tuning by a specialist.

Size and weight

The size of the gourd and the width and curve of the fretboard vary, although not the length of the latter. It is important to choose an instrument that reflects the size of the player and his handspan.

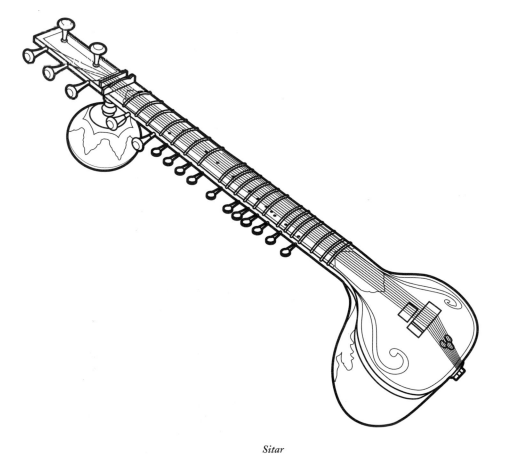

Sitar

OTHER STRING INSTRUMENTS

	Purchase price new	Second-hand availability	Maintenance	Weight	Ease of Learning	Is a small version available?
LUTE	♪♪	♪♪	♪♪	♪♪♪	♪♪	YES
MANDOLIN	♪♪♪♪	♪♪♪♪	♪♪♪	♪♪♪♪♪	♪♪♪♪	NO
UKULELE	♪♪♪♪♪	♪♪♪♪	♪♪♪♪♪	♪♪♪♪♪	♪♪♪♪	NO
BANJO	♪♪♪♪	♪♪♪♪	♪♪♪♪	♪♪♪♪	♪♪♪♪	YES
BALALAIKA	♪♪♪♪	♪♪♪♪	♪♪♪♪	♪♪♪♪	♪♪♪♪	YES

The lute, mandolin, ukulele, banjo and balalaika are fretted stringed instruments that don't regularly feature on lists of instruments offered for tuition in school. Private teachers specializing in them are also few and far between, although many teacher-players may play one as a second or third instrument. The fact that they are less commonly taught may give them added appeal to some children. Children are less likely to choose these instruments unless they have specific exposure to them.

Lute

The name and shape derive from the Arabic *ud*, an instrument that came to Europe in the Middle Ages. The sitar (see pages 56–57) developed in northern India at the same time as the lute. The lute's popularity, which extended for 150 years from the late 15th century, can be com-

Lute

pared to that of the guitar today. By the end of the 17th century, the lute's days as a popular instrument were numbered, not least because its dynamic range is small. The instrument is found in numerous forms, but the basic shape resembles a large bowl-backed mandolin. The lute usually has between 15 and 24 strings, which are plucked. A difficult instrument to tune and quite expensive to purchase

Mandolin

A member of the lute family, this small instrument is found in two versions: the Neapolitan or bowl-backed mandolin and the flat-backed mandolin. The former is referred to in Louis de Bernieres' novel *Captain Corelli's Mandolin*. The mandolin has eight strings, tuned in pairs: G G–D D–A A–E E. Both versions of the instrument are played with a plectrum, or plastic pick. Mandolins are modestly priced and quite robust.

Ukulele

A cross between a mandolin and a guitar, the ukulele is a small instrument that looks like a miniature guitar. The soprano form with four strings tuned A–E–C–G is small and highly portable. There are three larger instruments with up to eight strings. Soprano versions can be purchased cheaply and are easy to look after.

Banjo

Originating in Africa, the banjo is a long-necked, four-, five- or six-stringed instrument. It was taken to North America by slaves, from whence it moved to Europe. The five stringed model is most common, with the tuning G–D–B–G–D. The instrument is similar in size to the mand-

Banjo

olin but with a longer neck. The body of the instrument is covered with skin, or on contemporary instruments a plastic membrane, that increases resonance. Banjos are modestly priced and easy to care for.

Balalaika

Not only used for folk music, this lute-like Russian instrument is popular in bands and orchestras in Russia. It has a triangular body and long neck with three strings tuned according to the size of the instrument, region and genre of music played. A common tuning is E–E–A. The instrument is relatively expensive.

Learning these instruments

Although children starting out on any of these instruments benefit from a good teacher, the ukulele and banjo in particular may be self-taught. They could all be interesting second instruments for children who have already made good progress on another instrument. All are relatively light to carry, with the soprano ukulele being the smallest, lightest and most portable of all.

WOODWIND FAMILY

Woodwind instruments derive their name from the simple fact that they were once all made of wood and make a sound when wind is blown through them. Saxophones, made of metal, were added to the family in the mid-19th century, and since the beginning of the 20th century most flutes and piccolos have been constructed from metal. Clarinets and saxophones employ single reeds, a thin piece of cane that sets the column of air vibrating; oboes and bassoons have double reeds. Flutes, piccolos and fifes do not have a reed. The recorder, flute, oboe, B flat clarinet, bassoon and saxophone are the most commonly taught woodwind instruments.

Where to hear the instruments

In the Classical orchestra two flutes, oboes, clarinets and bassoons comprised a woodwind section. When the orchestra expanded in the 19th century, the woodwind often doubled, or additional members of the family were added according to the composer's preference. Orchestral music for woodwind instruments is a mixture of technically demanding passages and much simpler writing. The military band and symphonic windband extend the repertoire of woodwind instruments, unlike jazz ensembles, which generally only use saxophones, B flat clarinet and flute.

What makes a woodwind player?

The production of sound on clarinets and saxophones is similar; so, too, is sound production on the double reed instruments. This means many woodwind players perform on more than one instrument of the family. Most players concentrate on one instrument until they have achieved some degree of mastery before moving to a second or subsequent instrument. Woodwind players have to cope with instruments that, although quite robust when compared with strings, rely on complex playing mechanisms, and often a wooden construction sensitive to temperature and moisture. Reeds are a permanent source of anxiety for most professional players, who are forever in search of the perfect reed that allows access to low and high notes, loud and quiet passages with equal ease. Children starting on woodwind instruments may experience some discomfort with tired lips. A good teacher guards against excessive discomfort while strength builds up during the early stages of learning.

OCARINA

OCARINA

PURCHASE PRICE NEW ♩♩♩♩

SECOND-HAND AVAILABILITY ♩♩♩♩♩

MAINTENANCE ♩♩♩♩♩

WEIGHT ♩♩♩♩

EASE OF LEARNING ♩♩♩♩♩

IS A SMALL VERSION AVAILABLE? YES

This folk-music instrument dates back thousands of years and is found in various forms across a range of cultures. The ocarina has the same basic range of notes as the recorder and blends well with that instrument. Perhaps its greatest advantage over the recorder is that when blown excessively hard it doesn't make a sound, whereas a recorder emits a shrill, piercing note.

Ocarina

Repertoire

In addition to the folk repertoire for which it was created, a wide range of arrangements of all types of music have been published for the ocarina.

How it is played

The modern version of the instrument, often made of plastic, is potato shaped and fits neatly into a small cupped hand. It can be worn on a lanyard (a cord with an attached hook), or around the neck. When blown, the instrument makes its sound in the same way as the recorder (see page 63).

Learning the ocarina

It is an easy instrument on which to make a sound, and beginners learn simple tunes quickly. It is available in different sizes.

Aptitude and temperament

The ocarina is an ideal starter instrument for young children. They are able to explore issues associated with music-making and so make a more informed decision about which instrument to move on to.

Cost and maintenance

One of the cheapest musical instruments available, the ocarina has no running costs other than perhaps an occasional replacement lanyard.

Size and weight

Ocarinas come in a range of sizes, the smallest being no bigger than a matchbox and weighing only a few grams.

DESCANT RECORDER

As well as being fun to play, the recorder is a serious musical instrument. In the 16th and 17th centuries, recorder consorts – comprising sopranino, descant, treble, tenor and bass recorders – played music specially written for them. It is an easy instrument on which to make a sound and so a good place to start learning to play. Most schools have a supply of recorders.

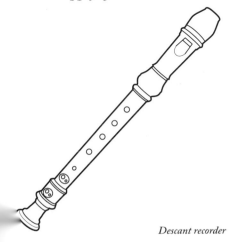

Descant recorder

Repertoire

The repertoire for the recorder is huge, extending from music composed for it as a consort instrument to arrangements of contemporary pop music and film scores.

How it is played

Recorders are made of wood or plastic. The player places the mouthpiece between his lips and blows gently into it. Players vary the note by opening and closing holes in the instrument with the fingers.

Learning the recorder

The recorder is often used as a whole-class instrument in schools, and there is plenty of contemporary music written for such groups. Like all instruments, it is difficult to play really well.

Aptitude and temperament

The recorder is a favourite with children because, like the ocarina, it's easy to make a sound using it. For the same reason, it is sometimes less popular with parents.

Cost and maintenance

The price is modest and consequently the second-hand market almost non-existent. It is worth paying more than the minimum for an instrument with better tone and intonation. Running costs are minimal.

Size and weight

The instrument fits inside a coat pocket and weighs no more than a few grams.

FLUTE

This popular instrument was originally made out of wood, but today most are manufactured from metal. The instrument is a very popular choice for learning at school, particularly among girls. Although it is unlikely to be a serious consideration when starting lessons, bear in mind that as a child flautist gets older, there may be some competition within a school for places in a band or orchestra because of its popularity.

Also in the family

The piccolo, a smaller, higher pitched version of the flute used by orchestral composers to provide particularly high notes, is not a beginner's instrument. The flute family also includes alto and bass instruments to which players may extend their expertise having mastered the flute. These are used principally in flute choirs or for particular effects in orchestral scoring.

Repertoire

Flute parts are written for orchestra, windbands, wind quintets and jazz ensembles, and the instrument's huge repertoire covers many styles of music. It can feature as a solo instrument and be accompanied by piano.

How it is played

The player holds the instrument to one side of the head and blows air across the mouthpiece, a hole near one end of the instrument, in order to make a sound. Keys are lifted and depressed to play notes of different pitches. The modern transverse flute began to replace the recorder as the orchestral instrument of choice in the times of Bach and Handel at the beginning of the 18th century.

Learning the flute

The flute is ideal for children aged 9–11 years and onwards. Some teachers encourage younger children to begin on the fife before graduating to the flute. Flutes with curved head joints allow younger players with a shorter reach to start on the instrument. Once a sound has been established, the player must get used to holding the flute to one side of the head. Most models of flute use plateau keywork, in which the player's fingers press keys which in turn cover the holes. This means the player's fingers don't have to be particularly big to make notes.

Aptitude and temperament

Although few find it impossible to make a sound on a flute, children occasionally find it is initially difficult to do so. To some extent, this depends on physical make-up: the shape of the mouth and jaw combined with the position and development of teeth. An experienced teacher can usually tell by looking at a potential pupil whether or not he is likely to find the instrument easy or more difficult.

Cost and maintenance

The purchase price is relatively modest and the second-hand market good. Running costs include occasional maintenance, which is best left to a professional repairer or flute teacher: parents and children should not attempt to tighten or loosen the many small visible screws that adjust or hold parts of the instrument in place.

Size and weight

Flutes are light and easy to carry and the cases are unobtrusive. Flutes are available with a curved head joint which reduces the total length. The benefit for younger children is that they can reach out far enough to hold the instrument (this may be difficult with a regular flute).

Flute

OBOE

OBOE

PURCHASE PRICE NEW	♩♩♩
SECOND-HAND AVAILABILITY	♩♩♩
MAINTENANCE	♩♩♩
WEIGHT	♩♩♩
EASE OF LEARNING	♩♩♩♩
IS A SMALL VERSION AVAILABLE? NO	

This instrument developed in Baroque times and is best suited to orchestral and ensemble work, including the wind quintet. It has a place, too, in modern windbands and military bands. When played well, the oboe's haunting quality and pastoral sounds make it very special. Good oboe players are scarce and therefore highly sought-after.

Also in the family

Other instruments belonging to the oboe family include the cor anglais and oboe d'amore. The cor anglais is an orchestral instrument which is often taken up by oboists, but only after they become proficient on the oboe. The oboe d'amore is similarly not a beginners' instrument and features chiefly in orchestral music of the 18th century.

Repertoire

The oboe is at its best playing music written for it rather than transcriptions of other works. Its core repertoire is the music of the Baroque period and orchestral works of the Classical and Romantic eras. It is less often used in jazz or popular music. In windbands and concert bands oboists play arrangements of lighter music.

How it is played

Sound is made on this instrument by placing its double reed between the lips and blowing air through the narrow gap between the reeds into the instrument. The sensitivity of the reed is essential to the sound. Notes are varied by lifting and depressing the fingers, or keys, to cover holes along the instrument's length.

Learning the oboe

This is perhaps the hardest woodwind instrument for beginners because of its double reed, which is easily damaged, and the sensitivity of the reed in relation to sounding notes. Size of hand is impor tant, too, for covering holes in the instrument. The clarinet and bassoon share this feature whereas the flute does not. Age 10–11 is probably the earliest starting point. Finding a good reed is, for the novice player, largely a matter of luck.

Aptitude and temperament

Beginner oboists need encouragement and support, since with novice players the instrument tends to produce a coarse and rather harsh, penetrating sound. Developing control and mastery of the sound and tone can be difficult and it is not for those who give up easily. The instrument may appeal to a child who is more interested in 'serious' music, or to someone who can enjoy playing one sort of music on the oboe, and other styles on another instrument or through singing.

Cost and maintenance

The price of a beginner's instrument is relatively modest, although a little more expensive than either a flute or clarinet. Instruments suitable for beginners can be made of synthetic materials which are more durable than wood. There are comparatively few good oboes on the second-hand market. Running costs include occasional maintenance (which should be carried out by an experienced technician) and regular replacement reeds, since beginners can go through a great many. Experienced, older players may make or prepare their own reeds. This is an exacting task and not for the beginner.

Size and weight

The instrument is small and not heavy for a child to carry. For travelling and storage, the oboe fits into a compact lightweight case.

Oboe

CLARINET

CLARINET

PURCHASE PRICE NEW ♩♩♩♩
SECOND-HAND AVAILABILITY ♩♩♩♩♩
MAINTENANCE ♩♩♩♩
WEIGHT ♩♩♩♩♩
EASE OF LEARNING ♩♩♩♩
IS A SMALL VERSION AVAILABLE? YES

Often described as one of the most versatile instruments, the clarinet was originally made of African hardwood, boxwood or grenadilla, and thus was sensitive to the impact of the warm moist air blown by a player through the instrument. If the wood were not properly seasoned, or subsequently looked after, the instrument could easily split. Modern high-quality instruments are still made of wood, but a range of instruments made of artificial materials are ideal for beginners and can be played to a high standard as well.

Also in the family

The clarinet family includes alto, bass, contra-alto and contrabass instruments. The sound is made in a similar way with all. As well as the regular B flat clarinet which suffices beginners for several years, orchestral players employ an A clarinet. These instruments are essentially the same – the A model is simply pitched one semitone lower.

Repertoire

The clarinet developed in the 18th century and was a favourite of Mozart, who wrote a concerto for it. It is a member of the symphony orchestra and of equal value in jazz ensembles, windbands and chamber music. Gershwin's Rhapsody in Blue features the clarinet in its famous opening bars.

How it is played

The regular B flat instrument must be assembled each time it is played, and the reed attached to the mouthpiece. The mouthpiece goes into the player's mouth with the reed resting on the lower lip, which is held over the bottom teeth. By closing his mouth around the reed and mouthpiece and blowing air between the reed and the mouthpiece, the player sets the column of air inside the instrument vibrating. This produces sound. The reed is fragile, and the slightest damage affects its ability to vibrate and thus the sound quality, or even the potential to produce a sound at all. Plastic reeds are generally regarded as a poor substitute for the re thing by more experienced players because they are less sensitive.

Learning the clarinet

The clarinet is a popular choice for beginners and the sound is fairly easy to make over the whole range of the instrument. Beginners learn the B flat instrument or its relatively new companions, the Kinder-Klari (pitched in E flat) or Lyons C clarinet, which are made lighter and smaller for children.

Aptitude and temperament

Many players find the clarinet an easy instrument to take up after playing the recorder. The 6–10 age range is probably a good time to start learning. Developing fluency and good intonation is more difficult and requires commitment and persistence.

Cost and maintenance

The cost of either a new B flat , Kinder-Klari, or Lyons C clarinet is relatively modest. There is a thriving second-hand market. Running costs include occasional maintenance, which should always be undertaken by an experienced technician, and reeds. The reed is quite fragile and easily damaged. Beginners seem to eat reeds! Instruments made of synthetic materials are designed to tolerate being less well looked after than the wooden models.

Size and weight

Full-sized clarinets are not too heavy, even when carried in the case, and children of eight years and up find them easy to transport. The smaller, lighter Kinder-Klari and Lyons C models are gaining in popularity with younger beginners.

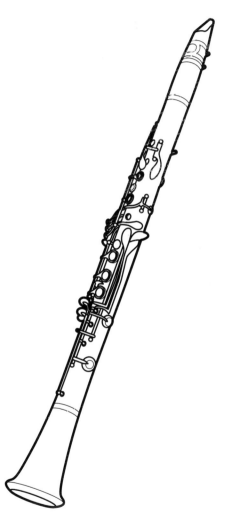

Clarinet

BASSOON

BASSOON

PURCHASE PRICE NEW	♪♪♪
SECOND-HAND AVAILABILITY	♪♪♪
MAINTENANCE	♪♪♪
WEIGHT	♪♪♪
EASE OF LEARNING	♪♪♪
IS A SMALL VERSION AVAILABLE?	YES

The bassoon developed in the Baroque era, taking its place in the orchestra of the Classical period. Although found in military and windbands, the instrument is little used in popular music and jazz. Bassoon players are always in demand. They can be sure of a place in any ensemble, providing as they do the bass part for a woodwind group.

Repertoire

The bassoon is equally at home in pieces written for orchestra, windband or wind quintet. One famous piece is in the opening bars of The Rite of Spring by Stravinsky. Ensemble parts played by this bass instrument may be a little less demanding than those played by higher pitched instruments. Mini bassoons sound a fifth interval above the written note, and so music has to be specially arranged to accommodate them. As for all instruments, sheet music is widely available: ask a teacher to direct you to a good retailer.

How it is played

Sound is made by placing the double reed between the lips and blowing air through the narrow gap between the reeds and into the instrument, as with the oboe (see pages 66–67). The instrument is designed to be played sitting down, and the player uses either a spike attached to the end of the instrument or a sling around the neck to lift the weight of the bassoon away from the hands and arms. It is possible, using a sling, to play standing up, and thus possible to march playing a bassoon.

Learning the bassoon

Mini bassoons are light in weight and are suitable for primary school children aged 8–11. The full-size bassoon is probably more suited to children aged 10–11, or older. Encouraging beginners to start on a full-size instrument can be a problem.

Aptitude and temperament

Holes in the instrument are covered by the player's fingers rather than parts of the mechanism, making the size of the learner's hand vital to achieving correct notes. This can make learning difficult for a younger or smaller child. Players gain a real sense of leadership by providing the bass to an ensemble.

Cost and maintenance

Modern beginners' bassoons, like oboes and clarinets, are made of artificial materials. A new bassoon is a significant purchase; more expensive than a flute, clarinet or oboe, but modest in cost when compared to a quality stringed instrument. The second-hand market is weak. Running costs include occasional maintenance, which should always be carried out by an experienced technician, and reeds. New players may go through reeds at a considerable rate.

Size and weight

Bassoons are relatively heavy and the cases are quite large. A full-size instrument in its case might be too cumbersome for children under ten years or so to carry. Mini bassoons are made smaller and lighter to suit younger children.

Bassoon

SAXOPHONE

SAXOPHONE	
PURCHASE PRICE NEW	♩♩♩
SECOND-HAND AVAILABILITY	♩♩♩
MAINTENANCE	♩♩♩
WEIGHT	♩♩♩
EASE OF LEARNING	♩♩♩
IS A SMALL VERSION AVAILABLE?	NO

A comparatively modern instrument, the saxophone was invented by Belgian instrument maker Adolph Sax in the mid 19th century. Despite having a metal body, it is classed as a member of the woodwind family of instruments. The saxophone's image as a 'cool' instrument to play makes it a popular choice for many children. The sounds are relatively easy to make and progress for beginners can be quite rapid.

Also in the family

Most beginners start on the alto or tenor saxophone, but there is a complete family of instruments, including soprano, baritone and bass. The alto, tenor and baritone saxophones are the most widely played, although the soprano has grown in popularity. The fingering for all saxophones is essentially the same, although the technique for producing sound varies.

Repertoire

In most people's minds, the saxophone is associated with jazz, although the instrument was invented before jazz evolved and so it can be used as a classical instrument or to play pieces in a more popular style. The saxophone features occasionally in orchestral music but it is most at home in the windband, jazz big band or jazz ensemble. It can also be heard in pop and rock.

How it is played

The saxophone combines a clarinet-like mouthpiece with a conical metal body. The instrument changes register at the octave (eighth tone of a scale or run of notes) like the flute and bassoon (and unlike the clarinet which changes register at the 12th note of the scale). The octave register change makes fingerings exactly the same for lower and higher notes, which may aid beginners. Saxophonists wear a strap or sling which enables them to take the weight of the instrument on the shoulders rather than the arms and thus play sitting or standing.

Learning the saxophone

This is an attractive instrument for beginners and also for clarinetists, who often move over to it, finding it similar to play. The alto saxophone in E flat is the most popular model for beginners. Children are sometimes encouraged to start on the B flat soprano saxophone, available in the familiar curved shape or straight (the latter looks rather like a clarinet). The danger for clarinet players is that they learn to make the sound in the same way as for the clarinet, not least because they copy their peers playing the clarinet. In the long term this prevents a player from developing the best embouchure (shape of the mouth and lips).

Aptitude and temperament

The instrument's construction means that holes are covered by parts of the mechanism rather than fingers, making the size of the player's hand almost immaterial. For beginners, this can be quite an advantage, as can the fact that sound is produced quite readily, and playing notes over the full range of the instrument is not too difficult. Be wary if a child is seduced by the 'cool' nature of the instrument. The thriving second-hand market is due in part to the number of children attracted to the instrument who give up when they find that, like most instruments, playing is never as easy as a professional makes it look.

Cost and maintenance

The purchase price is relatively modest, and there is a strong second-hand market for saxophones. Running costs include occasional maintenance by a professional, a sling or strap and reeds. Beginners may go through reeds at a great rate.

Size and weight

Alto saxophones are quite weighty to carry, and so children don't generally feel comfortable holding or transporting them until at least eight or nine years of age. Only larger, stronger or older children might be able to tackle the tenor, which is heavier still.

Saxophone

BRASS FAMILY

Although there are many brass instruments in this extended family, only the trumpet and cornet, baritone, tenor and French horns, euphonium and tenor trombone are commonly taught to beginners. Instruments belonging to the brass family make sound when air is blown through a detachable metal mouthpiece into a metal tube. The player uses three or four valves – or on the trombone a slide – to alter the length of the metal tube and this, combined with different lip tensions and air pressure, produces notes of different pitch. Well-played brass instruments have the power to cut through an orchestral or big-band texture. They offer fanfare, pomp and majesty, or melancholy, as in 'The Last Post', played to commemorate the loss of lives in war.

Where to hear the instruments

Brass instruments are played in brass bands, military and marching bands, orchestras, big bands, jazz bands and many other ensembles, with some instruments, such as the tenor and baritone horn and euphonium, used mainly in bands rather than as orchestral instruments. A substantial quantity of music has also been written for individual instruments and piano. Orchestral brass players follow a musical path distinct from brass band players, but at the earliest stages of learning such divisions are less important.

World of brass

Brass bands have a musical culture and life all their own. There are many high quality brass bands and most run junior and training bands for children, who may join sometimes as complete beginners and learn from scratch as part of an ensemble. Brass bands play in competitions against one another with their own leagues. Competition playing can help to drive up standards.

What makes a brass player?

Brass players often stick together. They tend to have a 'can do' attitude to playing that perhaps stems from their ability to drown out in sheer volume any other orchestral section. The brass player can take her instrument out of the case and start playing while the woodwind player is putting her instrument together and searching for a reed, and the string player is trying to tune up. Musically, brass players, particularly on trumpets and horns, learn to deal with transposition, producing sounds that differ from the musical notation. Children starting on brass may experience some discomfort such as sore fingers or tired lips. A good teacher will guard against excessive discomfort while strength is built up during the early stages of learning.

CORNET AND TRUMPET

CORNET AND TRUMPET	
PURCHASE PRICE NEW	♪♪♪♪
SECOND-HAND AVAILABILITY	♪♪♪
MAINTENANCE	♪♪♪♪
WEIGHT	♪♪♪♪
EASE OF LEARNING	♪♪♪
IS A SMALL VERSION AVAILABLE?	NO

These are the smallest and most popular instruments of the brass family, for their majestic sound and appealing gleam. Both cornet and trumpet have three valves and sound is produced in a similar way. The cornet has the same range of notes as a trumpet. Progress on the trumpet usually comes rapidly and so it often makes a good choice for beginners.

Cornet

Also in the family

The pocket trumpet is a miniaturized version of the standard B flat trumpet. Although something of a novelty item and not for beginners, experienced players find it useful for practice sessions. The flugelhorn, often heard in jazz ensembles, has a more conical bore (the tube into which air is blown) than the trumpet and plays lower pitched notes more readily. This, too, is not really a beginners' instrument; players tend to transfer easily once they have mastered the basics.

Repertoire

Music written for the trumpet is found from the Baroque period onwards, and the instrument features in the orchestral music of Haydn, Mozart and Beethoven through the Romantic era to the 20th century and present day. The trumpet is also found in pieces played by wind-bands, marching bands, military bands and jazz ensembles of all kinds. The cornet is more strongly associated with the brass band and military band.

How it is played

Different pitches are produced by a combination of pressing valves and using the lips to vibrate air blown through the mouthpiece in different ways. The harmonic series (see glossary, page 116–19) provides the basic notes of the instrument; players operate valves that access other pieces of tubing of differing lengths to find notes between the harmonics. Gaining mastery of this combination of harmonics and valved notes is the essence of brass playing, and once fluent on the trumpet, a player can move fairly easily to a lower-pitched brass instrument.

Learning the cornet and trumpet

Learners enjoy the simplicity of the cornet and the trumpet. This may be as much to do with the instruments' relatively few valves (three) to press down in various combinations, as with the fact that the player produces a series of notes that are the natural harmonics produced by any vibrating object. Young children are often encouraged to start on the cornet which, with its more compact shape, is easier to hold and less tiring on the arms. The transition to trumpet is not usually difficult. Teachers may recommend a switch of instrument to beginners who find playing higher pitched notes on the trumpet difficult.

Aptitude and temperament

Success in playing the trumpet – indeed any brass instrument – depends on regular practice to 'keep one's lip in'. There are no shortcuts with this, and it is definitely not an instrument that can only be practised the day before a lesson or rehearsal. When you play a note on the trumpet everyone in the ensemble knows about it, so children starting the instrument need a degree of self-confidence.

Cost and maintenance

The purchase price of a new trumpet or cornet is relatively modest, and although the second-hand market is good, many parents prefer to buy a new one. Running costs include occasional maintenance, a mouthpiece and valve oil. Both cornet and trumpet can be damaged easily, and although most dents are fairly readily removed, resulting trips to the repairers can be costly over time. The detachable mouthpiece requires regular cleaning.

Size and weight

Both instruments are relatively light and easily portable in their cases by younger children. Modern instrument cases are durable as well as lightweight.

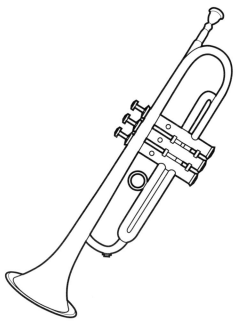

Trumpet

FRENCH HORN

Derived in France from the hunting horn during the middle of the 17th century, this instrument took its place in the classical orchestra of Mozart and Haydn. Composers use the French horn as a solo instrument, for example in the second movement of Tchaikovsky's Symphony No. 5.

Repertoire

The horn is used in music for military bands, windbands and, of course, the symphony orchestra, but doesn't feature routinely in jazz ensembles nor play in brass bands, where its place is taken by the E flat tenor horn (see page 82). In the orchestrations of the great Romantic composers, such as Brahms and Mahler, Wagner and Strauss, the horn comes into its own. It was adopted as readily by film composers in the late 20th century.

How it is played

Sound is produced in a similar way to that of other brass instruments. The player puts his hand in the bell of the instrument to support it and to change the pitch of some notes. This is called hand-stopping.

Learning the French horn

The French horn can be started at around 9–11 years, and is sometimes chosen by the teacher for a learner who started out on a different brass instrument and mastered some basic principles.

Aptitude and temperament

This is a difficult instrument to play – even French horn players say this. It is probably easier to play a wrong note by mispitching on the French horn than on any other brass instrument. The horn might best suit a child who perseveres, shrugging off mistakes with good humour. That said, French horn players are welcome in school and amateur orchestras where there is usually a short-age of good players.

Cost and maintenance

French horns are more expensive than trumpets or trombones, perhaps because they are more complicated to make and relatively few are sold, when compared with trumpet and trombone. The detach-able mouthpiece requires regular cleaning.

Size and weight

French horns can be heavy for a young person to carry, and the shape of most cases, which follow the contours of the instrument, make them quite cumber-some. Most children will not feel com-fortable handling and transporting the instrument until they reach the later years of primary school.

French horn

TROMBONE

The name 'trombone' derives from the Italian for large trumpet, and the instrument dates back to the Renaissance. Until the early 18th century it was known as a sackbut. This is the only member of the brass family that usually has a slide mechanism rather than valves, although a valved version is available. The most commonly played modern instrument is the tenor trombone in B flat. Although described as a B flat instrument it is not a transposing instrument, unlike the B flat trumpet: it sounds the notes as written on the stave.

Repertoire

The trombone repertoire ranges from the majestic to the comic, and most players find a musical style to suit them. Mozart wrote interesting parts for the trombone, for example, the 'tuba mirum' in his Requiem. Today the instrument features in music written for windband and orchestra, and improvises in jazz ensembles. Its ability to execute glissando, slide between notes, gives it an ability to produce comic as well as more threatening effects. The modern orchestral trombone plays music written for it in the bass clef. When playing music written for brass band, the player reads in the treble clef since in these settings the trombone is written for as a transposing instrument.

How it is played

The player changes the pitch of the note by moving the slide to the position of one of the notes in the harmonic series (see glossary, page 116–19) and adjusting her embouchure (the shape of the mouth and lips).

Learning the trombone

Although a slightly more difficult instrument to handle than the trumpet, the trombone is an easier one on which to make a sound. The instrument suits children aged 8–10 and older.

Aptitude and temperament

Brass instruments require energy and stamina, which most children have in abundance. Younger boys and all girls may have to come to terms with the fact that many of the notes played by the trombone are below the pitch at which they can sing. For most children this is not a problem.

Cost and maintenance

This is a modestly priced instrument. Although there is a good second-hand market, most parents prefer to buy a new one. The detachable mouthpiece should be cleaned regularly and the slide must be looked after very carefully, since it is easily dented or knocked out of true; without a free-moving slide it is impossible to play the instrument well.

Size and weight

The regular-sized trombone is quite large to carry around; consider this and the size of the child before booking lessons. A mini-format instrument makes learning easier – and physically more manageable – for younger children.

Trombone

TENOR HORN

TENOR HORN

PURCHASE PRICE NEW ♪♪

SECOND-HAND AVAILABILITY ♪♪♪♪

MAINTENANCE ♪♪♪

WEIGHT ♪♪♪

EASE OF LEARNING ♪♪♪

IS A SMALL VERSION AVAILABLE? NO

This instrument was invented in the middle of the 19th century as the alto voice in the saxhorn family developed by Adolphe Sax, creator of the saxophone. The name 'alto' was dropped in favour of tenor. Do not confuse this horn with the French horn. Music for the instrument is written in the treble clef.

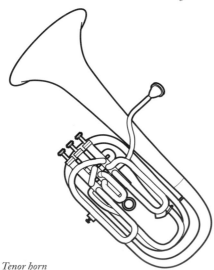

Tenor horn

Repertoire

The tenor horn does not figure in orchestral writing. Brass bands, however, are very welcoming, playing music from a broad range of musical styles and offering many performance opportunities. The tenor horn should be welcome in a windband or concert band.

How it is played

Children find this one of the easier brass instruments to start learning because it is simpler to pitch than the trumpet and cornet and requires a slightly more relaxed embouchure (shape of mouth and lips).

Learning the tenor horn

Many brass bands offer tuition that includes a beginner sitting in and being helped by more experienced players. For would-be players this can be an ideal way of finding out if they like the instrument.

Aptitude and temperament

Playing a brass band instrument allows children to become part of an ensemble. This might suit less confident children.

Cost and maintenance

New instruments are not too expensive and there is a steady second-hand market. They are easy to look after but the detachable mouthpiece requires regular cleaning.

Size and weight

The instrument is neither too heavy nor cumbersome for a child to hold or carry.

TUBA

TUBA	
PURCHASE PRICE NEW ♩♩♩♩	
SECOND-HAND AVAILABILITY ♩♩♩	
MAINTENANCE ♩♩♩	
WEIGHT ♩	
EASE OF LEARNING ♩♩	
IS A SMALL VERSION AVAILABLE? NO	

The tuba is similar in appearance to the euphonium, but bigger and of different origins. Although it is a large and somewhat unwieldy instrument, the tuba is always much in demand because it plays the bass part in ensembles. There is usually one tuba in an orchestra. Although it is large, the tuba's sound is soft, warm and smooth.

Tuba

Repertoire

Parts may be written for one tuba in an orchestra or several tubas in a brass band.

How it is played

The player rests the instrument on his knee, holding it with one hand while pressing the valves with the other. The embouchure (shape of the mouth and lips) is easier to master for the tuba than for many brass instruments.

Learning the tuba

Although not difficult for a learner player, this instrument may not be a first choice for beginners. Players often move to the tuba after learning the basics on a different brass instrument.

Aptitude and temperament

Ensemble parts played by this bass instrument may be a little less demanding than those played by higher pitched instruments.

Cost and maintenance

New instruments are expensive; more costly than a trumpet, French horn or trombone. Second-hand tubas are available, but must be checked carefully: inexpert repairs can result in loss of tone on certain notes.

Size and weight

This is a large and heavy instrument to carry – it is one of the heaviest instruments detailed in this book. Bear this in mind if your child is younger or slight in build.

BARITONE HORN

BARITONE HORN

PURCHASE PRICE NEW ♪♪♪

SECOND-HAND AVAILABILITY ♪♪♪♪

MAINTENANCE ♪♪♪

WEIGHT ♪♪♪

EASE OF LEARNING ♪♪♪

IS A SMALL VERSION AVAILABLE? NO

The baritone horn pitched in B flat is usually found in brass bands and windbands rather than orchestras. Like the tenor horn it 'speaks' more easily than the French horn, and is neither too heavy nor large to carry around. Also like the tenor horn, it belongs to the saxhorn family and its relations in the brass world are the trumpet and trombone: all three have a cylindrical bore (the tube into which air is blown).

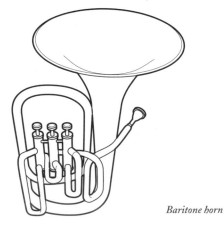

Baritone horn

Repertoire

The baritone's true repertoire is that of the brass band, which plays music from a broad range of musical styles. It is also welcome in windbands. Brass band music for baritone horn is written in the treble clef.

How it is played

The baritone horn is easier to pitch than the trumpet and cornet and uses a slightly more relaxed embouchure (shape of mouth and lips). Like the trumpet, cornet, tenor horn and euphonium, it has three valves.

Learning the baritone horn

Children find this one of the easier brass instruments on which to start learning, although many graduate from another brass instrument. Playing a brass band instrument means joining an ensemble which, in the way that it rehearses, is likely to look after members and make them feel part of a family group. Brass bands offer many performance opportunities.

Cost and maintenance

New instruments are not too expensive and there is a steady second-hand market. Baritone horns are easy to look after, but the detachable mouthpiece should be cleaned regularly.

Size and weight

The instrument is not too heavy for a child to hold, nor unwieldy to carry. It is smaller and more compact than the euphonium.

EUPHONIUM

This brass instrument looks like a large baritone horn (see page 84). One distinguishing feature is its wider bore (the tube into which air is blown), which is almost conical. For a big instrument, the sound is quite gentle. Most children are guided towards this instrument by a teacher once they have learnt the basics on a higher pitched brass instrument.

Euphonium

Repertoire

This is a wind and brass band instrument rather than an orchestral one. Orchestral euphonium parts are written in the bass clef, and brass band parts in the treble clef.

How it is played

The player holds the instrument with one hand and presses the valves with the other. It requires a strong embouchure (use of the mouth and lips) and good breath support.

Learning the euphonium

A teacher's recommendation is vital in guiding parents and children towards this instrument: she may be able to recognize a youngster with potential for whom the cornet or tenor horn is not the right instrument. Younger children learning to play euphonium have to produce notes below the range of their normal singing voices, although this is rarely a cause for concern.

Cost and maintenance

Euphoniums are relatively expensive. Brass instruments are not necessarily as robust as they may look, and dents are easily acquired. The detachable mouthpiece should be cleaned regularly, but maintenance should not be too costly.

Size and weight

The euphonium is large and heavy – there is no question of pretending you don't play it! Its case is also large. Less easy to carry around than many instruments, this choice may require parental assistance.

PERCUSSION FAMILY

earning a percussion instrument is a popular pastime for children, but less so for parents and neighbours, for obvious reasons. Boys in particular are drawn to the drum kit, although there is growing interest from girls. Interestingly, children rarely need reminding to practise the drums and seem to tap on any available surface. Percussion is more than a drum kit, however. The orchestral percussionist is expected to handle everything from bass drum to timpani (kettledrums), triangle, cymbals, glockenspiel, marimba and even piano. Playing a large number of percussion instruments demands a range of skills and the development of expertise on a par with any other instrument or family of instruments. This range of expertise can only be acquired over a period of time; mastering snare drum basics is simply the foundation of study.

Where to hear the instruments

Percussion is everywhere, from classical works for the orchestra and film soundtracks through military and marching bands to jazz, folk and traditional ensembles, pop and especially rock music. Orchestral percussion instruments include tubular bells, glockenspiel, xylophone and vibraphone, and instruments used in Latin and jazz music include the guiro, cuica and berimbao.

Learning to read music

Many children learning percussion, especially drum kit, simply want to play pieces they already know, and see little point in learning to read from notation. This is a false economy. Do check that a percussion teacher can read music as well as drum notation and that he teaches this to children as part of the process of learning the instrument.

What makes a percussionist?

The kit player is responsible for keeping a band in time, and almost all percussion players require a clear conviction of purpose that enables them to come in on the right note at the right time. While an aptitude for this is shared with all instruments, false entries are more noticeable on a loud percussion instrument than on quieter woodwind.

ORCHESTRAL &
CLASSROOM PERCUSSION

The orchestral percussionist is expected to be able to play everything that makes a sound by being struck or shaken, and so the learner interested in playing in the percussion section of an orchestra needs practice on everything from triangle to vibraphone. Percussion teachers tend to fall into two groups: those who teach the drum kit and those who teach a broad range of percussion instruments. When engaging a private teacher, make sure her skills match the musical requirements of your would-be orchestral percussionist. There is no chart here to guide you in purchasing instruments because they are mostly provided for beginners.

Repertoire

German music educator Carl Orff developed a curriculum for classroom music-teaching using pitched and unpitched classroom percussion instruments, and in many schools children have the opportunity to play the xylophone (wooden bars), glockenspiel or metallophone. Percussion parts are not only written for orchestra and bands, but for percussion ensembles. However, opportunities for children to join such a group may be limited because of a shortage of percussion teachers or lack of access to a full range of instruments, many of which are very expensive to buy.

How they are played

Percussion instruments are hit or shaken to make a sound. They divide into two categories: those that play a recognizable pitch, or more than one pitch, and those that do not.

Learning orchestral percussion

Most children encounter percussion instruments as part of classroom music-making from preschool age onwards. Large orchestral percussion instruments, such as timpani and marimba, are usually only available at school or orchestra rehearsals. Most large percussion instruments are not readily transportable, nor can they be easily accommodated at home, making home practise difficult.

Aptitude and temperament

Some learners feel less than comfortable mastering a range of percussion instruments and might be better directed to concentrate on the drum kit (see pages 90–91). Exam boards may require experience across a wide range of percussion instruments or offer more focused opportunities. Explore the options with a teacher.

Cost and maintenance

One advantage for would-be percussionists is that most of the instruments and equipment required are supplied by a band, ensemble or orchestra. Learners may be asked initially to provide no more than one or more pairs of sticks. The greatest risk of damage to percussion instruments comes from transportation from rehearsal to concert and back.

Size and weight

Many orchestral percussion instruments – timpani, bass drum, marimba, vibraphone – are too large to accommodate at home, and too heavy to transport easily. In addition to the larger instruments there is a wide range of lighter, hand-held percussion instruments, including for example Latin American percussion instruments, such as the guiro, maracas and cabasa.

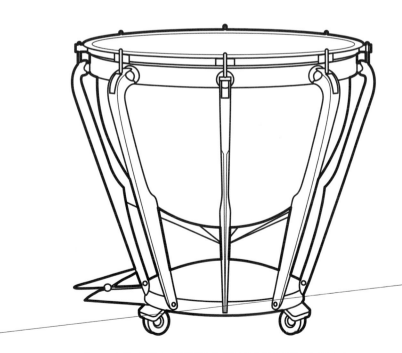

Timpani

DRUM KIT

DRUM KIT

PURCHASE PRICE NEW ♪♪♪♪

SECOND-HAND AVAILABILITY ♪♪♪♪

MAINTENANCE ♪♪♪

WEIGHT ♪♪♪♪

EASE OF LEARNING ♪♪♪

IS A SMALL VERSION AVAILABLE? YES

The basic drum kit includes a bass drum played with a foot pedal, a snare drum, two or three tom toms, a ride cymbal and a hi-hat (two cymbals operated by a floor pedal). Rock musicians often have additional drums. Electronic kits date from the early 1970s, and recent developments include numerous sophisticated features of music technology. Written music for drum kits and electronic kits employs a series of symbols additional to conventional Western music notation.

Repertoire

This is extensive, including everything from light classical works through jazz to most categories of pop music. The snare drum is written for as part of the orchestra and as an instrument in military and marching bands. Drummers in pop groups usually memorize music, but as with bass guitar and keyboard players, those who learn to read from notation or chord symbols may gain access to a broader repertoire.

How it is played

The kit is much harder to play well than it looks, both in terms of sounds made and timing. Basic stick technique comes from learning the snare drum. Drum sticks come in a range of sizes and strengths. Wire brushes are sometimes used to create a particular effect. Kit players have to learn to control and co-ordinate their arm and leg movements individually.

Learning drum kit

Some percussion teachers work exclusively on kit; others include pitched and/or other percussion instruments in lessons. Children who learn drum kit need to practise at home, which raises noise issues. Practice pads for kit work are cheap to purchase and reduce the impact on a household and neighbours. A potentially more expensive option is an electronic kit, which can be played silently to the outside world, yet sounds terrific to the player wearing headphones. Check that the teacher is happy with this option before going ahead.

Aptitude and temperament

Playing the kit is a very physical activity. It requires a combination of physical strength and stamina as well as coordination and a sense of rhythm. Learners who use practice pads must be disciplined in order to be satisfied with the lack of sound.

Cost and maintenance

Drum kits can be expensive, particularly good quality, robust instruments, and carrying cases are sometimes sold separately, adding to the cost. Sticks and drum heads need to be replaced regularly, as do floor stands for mounting drums (easily overlooked when packing the instrument away for transportation). Electronic kits cost the same or more than an acoustic kit, varying according to quality.

Size and weight

Drum kits take up a good amount of space and need time both to set up and to dismantle. They can be difficult to transport, so pupils usually play instruments provided by the school. Parents should prepare for the day they are required to help carry the unwieldy kit around, which might necessitate a change of car.

Drum kit

STEEL PANS

Originating from the island of Trinidad in the West Indies, steel pans developed as an inexpensive way of making music by fashioning instruments from discarded oil drums. They became commercially available in the 1940s and are popular in schools, especially in areas with a West Indian population. Steel pans are the only new chromatic instrument (on which notes can be played in intervals of a semitone) to be invented in the 20th century.

Repertoire

The complete family of pans includes instruments of varying size, pitch and range of notes, including lead, or tenor pans, seconds (altos), cello and bass instruments. Music is written or arranged for the family of pans to play as a band, although tenor pans in particular also play solo or with other instruments. The repertoire encompasses all styles of music from calypso and jazz to Bach.

How they are played

Players usually stand and strike the pan using two beaters, one in each hand. Pan players often work from a form of notation when learning a new piece, but may learn and perform music from memory, too.

Learning the pans

Pans are usually learned through a combination of an individual or small group lessons and weekly full group rehearsals. A typical band has six to ten players, but can be much larger. Bands often include a non-pitched percussion section or an electronically generated percussion backing.

Aptitude and temperament

Playing pans is very much a group activity, and many steel bands give a large number of public performances. This has the advantage of boosting a player's self-esteem and presentation skills. It brings also the potential disadvantage of taking up large amounts of time in the evenings and weekends.

Cost and maintenance

In most cases instruments are provided by a school. Individuals are neither expected, nor required, to buy their own pan. A single chromed pan can cost as much as a flute or clarinet.

Size and weight

It may be possible to practise at home by taking home a lead pan, but most practising has to be done at school or in community groups.

History

It is probable that steel pans first came to public notice in the celebratory carnival held in Trinidad after the Second World War. Chromatic pans were developed in the 1930s which gave players access to all kinds of music.

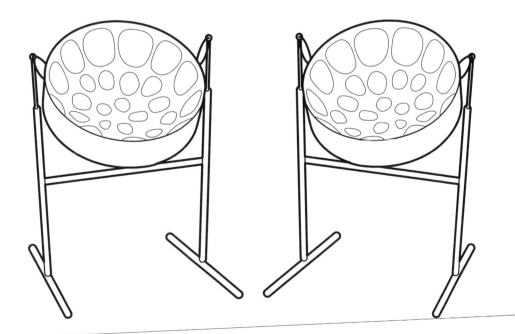

Steel pans

DJEMBE

DJEMBE	
PURCHASE PRICE NEW	♩♩♩♩
SECOND-HAND AVAILABILITY	♩♩♩
MAINTENANCE	♩♩♩
WEIGHT	♩♩♩
EASE OF LEARNING	♩♩♩
IS A SMALL VERSION AVAILABLE?	YES

A skin-covered drum played with the bare hands, the djembe comes from West Africa. The drum's popularity outside Africa has grown since the end of the 20th century and it is now taught widely in schools, where it may be used to help establish basic musical skills that can lead to further development on another instrument.

Djembe

Repertoire

Studying the djembe involves learning and memorizing a number of basic rhythmic patterns. Reading from musical notation is not an essential requirement.

How it is played

The player sits, or stands, and plays the drum with his hands.

Learning the djembe

This is an instrument to which children take readily, and although it can be the basis of a lifetime's study and exploration, the drum is more likely to provide an introduction to music-making from which learners move on to study another instrument. Playing as a part of a group can increase awareness of pulse and rhythm as well as improving coordination and self-esteem. You might find a school samba percussion band that offers the opportunity to acquire percussion skills as part of a large group.

Cost and maintenance

When children are given the opportunity to play djembe, instruments are usually provided and maintained by their school or local authority.

Size and weight

The djembe comes in various sizes, so a suitable one can usually be chosen to match the needs of the learner. Children are not expected to practice at home, so neither carrying the instrument nor noise levels at home are a concern.

TABLA

A popular percussion instrument, the tabla is used widely across all styles of North Indian music. The instrument consists of a pair of tuned, single-headed hand-played drums, and these are made in different sizes. Tabla is the name given to the higher pitched drum of the two.

Tabla

Repertoire

The tabla player performs classical music from Northern India. The player tunes his instrument to suit other instruments in an ensemble. Tabla may also be heard in Indian film soundtracks and, increasingly, in pop music.

How it is played

Players sit on the floor and play one drum with the strongest, or dominant, hand and the other drum with the second hand. Different sounds are made by using various parts of the hand, including the thumb, fingers, knuckle joints and heel of the hand.

Learning the tabla

Tabla teachers on the Indian subcontinent tend to belong to a school, or *gharana*, of teaching, meaning different players learn quite different technique. All learners, however, memorize the drums' various *bols*, or sounds, as well as set combinations of beats and rhythm cycles. Children without an understanding of Indian classical music may find tabla difficult to learn.

Cost and maintenance

Tabla are modestly priced, and running costs are also modest. It may be cheaper to buy a new set than replace heads and lacing.

Size and weight

Tabla are available in different sizes and so can be chosen to match the size and physique of the learner.

KEYBOARD
FAMILY

The family of keyboard instruments includes the pianoforte, usually referred to as a piano, and various types of electronic keyboard as well as harpsichord and organs. Grand, upright and electric pianos feature a single set of black and white keys, usually 88 covering seven octaves. Electronic keyboards often stop at five octaves. Harpsichords and organs tend to have more than one set of keys, or manuals (the term distinguishes keys depressed by the fingers from foot-operated pedals). The harpsichord makes a sound when 'jacks' pluck strings, and the pipe organ when air is blown through a pipe by an electronic blower.

Where to hear the instruments

The piano has a range of music wider than any other instrument, and is heard as a solo instrument and accompaniment in classical settings, jazz improvisation, and popular works of all types. In popular and modern classical music the range of sounds created by electronic keyboards is well explored. The pipe organ is best heard in church, the harpsichord and spinet in early music ensembles, while the Indian harmonium is heard largely in Indian classical music.

What makes a keyboard player?

Keyboard instruments require a number of complex skills. First, manual dexterity, although it is possible to play keyboards with restricted finger movement. Second, the expectation that both hands develop independence and strength. Finally, an ability simultaneously to read two lines of music written on two staves, each allocating contrasting lines and spaces to different note names. This is multi-tasking on a grand scale. The organ magnifies all this by having several manuals (keyboards), plus a pedal board that requires independent movement of each foot. Electronic keyboards help by doing some of the hard work for the player.

To make matters worse, most good pianists make playing look easy. They seem able to look away from the keyboard, perhaps taking in the audience and smiling, too. The answer is practice, and lots of it. Children and parents should be in no doubt that, while it is easy to make a sound on the piano (compared with an oboe or French horn, for example), the accumulation of skills required to perform a difficult piece should not be underestimated.

PIANO

PIANO

PURCHASE PRICE NEW ♩♩

SECOND-HAND AVAILABILITY ♩♩♩♩

MAINTENANCE ♩♩♩

WEIGHT ♩

EASE OF LEARNING ♩♩♩

IS A SMALL VERSION AVAILABLE? YES

Developed at the beginning of the 18th century, the piano is technically classed as a percussion instrument because its sound is made by hammers hitting strings when a player presses the keys. The basic form of the instrument has changed little since the middle of the 19th century, but the 20th century saw the growth of a broader range of instruments, including mini upright pianos and electric keyboards. A facility on the piano gives access to music written in a wide range of musical styles. For many learners and musicians piano becomes a second instrument – it has been described as the musician's maid-of-all-work.

Repertoire

The piano is used in all kinds of ensemble music-making or as a solo instrument. The range of pieces especially written for the piano is enormous, and the instrument can also be used to play music composed for other instruments, creating a repertoire larger than for any other instrument.

How it is played

When the player depresses a key, a hammer strikes a string, which resonates on a soundboard inside the frame. The pressure and speed at which the player presses the key determines the quality and dynamics of the sound. Foot pedals soften and sustain notes when depressed. Upright and grand pianos are essentially the same instrument. A good grand piano makes a significantly different sound from an upright.

Modern upright piano

Learning the piano

Lessons can start at an early age – as soon as a child's fingers are large and strong enough to depress the keys. More recent small uprights include a practice pedal that presses a felt bar against the strings, reducing practice volume. Silent pianos are also available, which can be played normally, or electronically with the player listening on headphones. Learner pianists have the advantage of not having to take their instrument with them and the disadvantage of having to play on whatever instrument is provided. Learning on a grand as opposed to an upright piano feels different, partly due to the visual perspective the player has when seated at the instrument. The majority of learners begin on an upright model and may transfer to a grand if the teacher has both, or if parents or school choose to provide one.

Aptitude and temperament

The piano is a difficult instrument to play well, albeit an easy instrument on which to make a sound. Playing requires simultaneous independent activity with each hand, something some children find difficult. Regular practice is a prerequisite of success, and so children with patience and perseverance prosper.

Cost and maintenance

The purchase price is relatively modest for a second-hand piano, and the market is strong. A quality upright may produce a better sound than a baby grand of poorer quality. When buying second-hand it is important to check that the instrument is either in tune or capable of being tuned to 'concert pitch' (when A above middle C is tuned to a frequency of 440 Hertz). This is particularly important if you plan to use the piano to accompany other instruments. Equally practically, look for active woodworm in second-hand instruments. Set the capital cost of a piano against its life expectancy: some 30 to 100 years or more. Running costs include occasional maintenance and regular tuning.

Size and weight

A small upright piano weighs about 200 kg (440 lb) and can be accommodated in most homes without too much difficulty. As a rule of thumb, the older the upright, the larger it will be. Since the 1970s, there has been a considerable increase in the development, manufacture and sales of small upright pianos designed for flats and small houses. Experienced piano movers, however, regularly tackle flights of stairs and, if necessary, can deliver instruments through upper floor windows. Grand pianos come in various sizes, from baby through 1.3 m (4ft 6in), 1.5 m (5 ft) and 1.6 m (5ft 6in) sizes up to full concert grand.

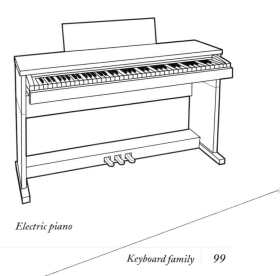

Electric piano

ELECTRONIC KEYBOARD

This is always a popular choice for young children: even relatively cheap instruments have a huge array of sounds, rhythms and features designed to entice a young player. The instrument's biggest advantage for many households is that it can be played with headphones. Parents may also wish to apply a drop of glue to the 'demo' button as an aid to sanity! Since the late 1980s, electric pianos have been manufactured similar in size to a small upright piano, with headphones and built-in speakers. Although these instruments go a long way to meet the needs of a pianist, they never provide quite the same sound quality and sensitivity of touch.

Repertoire

The unlimited repertoire includes all the music written for the instrument itself, arrangements of works of every type, plus the opportunity to play almost any part written for any instrument. In pop and rock circles, keyboard players often memorize music, but those who learn to read music gain access to a broader repertoire.

How it is played

The principal difference between the piano and an electronic keyboard is the way the sound is made. On the piano a note is sustained by holding a key down and gradually decays over 25–30 seconds. On an electronic keyboard a 'piano' sound may be constant until the key is released. The instruments require different performance techniques; with electronic keyboard touch sensitivity associated principally with the of the key.

Learning the keyboard

There are many published keyboard learning methods. electric pianos often have the facility to connect to allows learners to take ware applications that Children can record compositions and teacher. Some teachers stimulate practice quent teacher— by a weekly lesson

Learning the piano

Lessons can start at an early age – as soon as a child's fingers are large and strong enough to depress the keys. More recent small uprights include a practice pedal that presses a felt bar against the strings, reducing practice volume. Silent pianos are also available, which can be played normally, or electronically with the player listening on headphones. Learner pianists have the advantage of not having to take their instrument with them and the disadvantage of having to play on whatever instrument is provided. Learning on a grand as opposed to an upright piano feels different, partly due to the visual perspective the player has when seated at the instrument. The majority of learners begin on an upright model and may transfer to a grand if the teacher has both, or if parents or school choose to provide one.

Aptitude and temperament

The piano is a difficult instrument to play well, albeit an easy instrument on which to make a sound. Playing requires simultaneous independent activity with each hand, something some children find difficult. Regular practice is a prerequisite of success, and so children with patience and perseverance prosper.

Cost and maintenance

The purchase price is relatively modest for a second-hand piano, and the market is strong. A quality upright may produce a better sound than a baby grand of poorer quality. When buying second-hand it is important to check that the instrument is either in tune or capable of being tuned to 'concert pitch' (when A above middle C is tuned to a frequency of 440 Hertz). This is particularly important if you plan to use the piano to accompany other instruments. Equally practically, look for active woodworm in second-hand instruments. Set the capital cost of a piano against its life expectancy: some 30 to 100 years or more. Running costs include occasional maintenance and regular tuning.

Size and weight

A small upright piano weighs about 200 kg (440 lb) and can be accommodated in most homes without too much difficulty. As a rule of thumb, the older the upright, the larger it will be. Since the 1970s, there has been a considerable increase in the development, manufacture and sales of small upright pianos designed for flats and small houses. Experienced piano movers, however, regularly tackle flights of stairs and, if necessary, can deliver instruments through upper floor windows. Grand pianos come in various sizes, from baby through 1.3 m (4ft 6in), 1.5 m (5 ft) and 1.6 m (5ft 6in) sizes up to full concert grand.

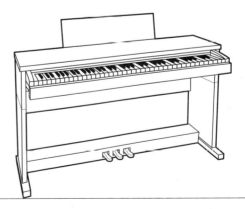

Electric piano

ELECTRONIC KEYBOARD

This is always a popular choice for young children: even relatively cheap instruments have a huge array of sounds, rhythms and features designed to entice a young player. The instrument's biggest advantage for many households is that it can be played with headphones. Parents may also wish to apply a drop of glue to the 'demo' button as an aid to sanity! Since the late 1980s, electric pianos have been manufactured similar in size to a small upright piano, with headphones and built-in speakers. Although these instruments go a long way to meet the needs of a pianist, they never provide quite the same sound quality and sensitivity of touch.

Repertoire

The unlimited repertoire includes all the music written for the instrument itself, arrangements of works of every type, plus the opportunity to play almost any part written for any instrument. In pop and rock circles, keyboard players often memorize music, but those who learn to read music gain access to a broader repertoire.

How it is played

The principal difference between the piano and an electronic keyboard is the way the sound is made. On the piano a note is sustained by holding a key down, and gradually decays over 25–30 seconds. On an electronic keyboard a 'piano' sound may be constant until the key is released. The instruments require different performance techniques; with an electronic keyboard touch sensitivity is associated principally with the velocity of the key.

Learning the keyboard

There are many published electronic keyboard learning methods. Keyboards and electric pianos often have disc drives, or the facility to connect to a computer. This allows learners to take advantage of software applications that support teaching. Children can record performances or compositions and e-mail them to a teacher. Some teachers encourage this to stimulate practice and enable more frequent teacher-pupil contact than offered by a weekly lesson. While there is no substitute for face-to-face teaching and learning, such developments show the way forward for many.

Aptitude and temperament

It is important that children and parents are clear from the outset whether they are learning the keyboard as an instrument in its own right or as a substitute piano. Learners should be prepared for teachers who insist that the piano must be learned first or that a keyboard is not an acceptable substitute for practice because of its different 'touch'.

Cost and maintenance

Keyboards are available at modest prices, whereas electric pianos are closer in price to acoustic pianos (see pages 98–99). The very smallest electronic keyboards are unlikely to be suitable for serious learning although they provide an ideal introduc-tion to keyboards for young children. Synthesizers offer something more than electronic keyboards and are, in many respects, less suitable for young beginners. Hidden costs may include headphones, stands, amplifier, software and a comput-er as well as increased electricity bills. Electronic keyboards and electric pianos never need tuning and should be reliable for many years.

Size and weight

Electronic keyboards come in a variety of sizes. Most have a five octave com-pass, which is sufficient for beginners. Electric pianos usually have the same 88 note range as an acoustic piano. Although they can be moved more easi-ly than an acoustic piano, they are designed to stay in one place most of the time. Keyboards are portable and may require a case.

Electronic keyboard

HARPSICHORD

A forerunner of the piano, the harpsichord often has two sets of keys, known as manuals, and its strings are plucked, rather than struck. The spinet is in essence a small harpsichord. Electronic versions of both spinet and harpsichord may be used in performance as a substitute for the real thing.

Harpsichord

Repertoire

This instrument is at its best when playing music written for it; most composers stopped so doing from Beethoven's time onward. A few contemporary composers write for the harpsichord, but the available contemporary repertoire is unlikely to appeal to most children.

How it is played

The harpsichord is played in a similar fashion to the piano. Players learn to work with a different 'touch' to other keyboard instruments.

Learning the harpsichord

Most children begin on the piano and then move to the harpsichord if it appeals to them. Few harpsichord teachers specialize in working with complete beginners.

Cost and maintenance

The harpsichord is an expensive instrument to purchase. The instruments need frequent tuning and most serious players take on this additional task themselves.

Size and weight

Although in shape they resemble a baby grand piano, harpsichords are much lighter because they have a wooden rather than an iron frame. The keys may be smaller than those of modern keyboard instruments. Size varies according to the region in which the instrument was made, but harpsichords are not scaled down for beginners.

ORGAN

ORGAN

PURCHASE PRICE NEW ♩

SECOND-HAND AVAILABILITY ♩♩

MAINTENANCE ♩♩♩

WEIGHT ♩♩

EASE OF LEARNING ♩♩♩

IS A SMALL VERSION AVAILABLE? NO

Whether electronic, pipe, or the blown-air, variety commonly found in churches, organs have one or more keyboards, known as manuals, and a pedal board as well, which makes playing a complex feat of coordination and technique. The electronic organ grew in popularity before the development of the electronic keyboard (see pages 100–101). The latter, which is more portable, is the more popular choice today.

Pipe organ

Repertoire

Music for pipe organs has often been written to suit the instrument's ecclesiastical setting. This has set an implicit restriction on the style of music able to be studied. Music for electronic instruments tends to be from the world of light entertainment, but these types of organs may also form part of a jazz ensemble.

How it is played

In order to play well, the learner must develop technical prowess similar to that of a pianist (see pages 98–99) while focusing on independent footwork, too.

Learning the organ

Playing the pipe organ almost certainly means practising in a church. Organists usually begin as piano students. Children enjoy playing the electronic version of the organ because its technology allows them to play a sophisticated piece almost from the outset.

Cost and maintenance

Church organs by their nature are not instruments bought or maintained at home. Electronic organs are less popular to buy than electronic keyboards (see pages 100–101).

Size and weight

Church organs do not move! Electronic organs are portable by comparison, but are not designed to be moved frequently.

INSTRUMENT SUMMARY CHART

This table summarizes in chart form key information about each of the instruments profiled on pages 40-113. Use it to help you compare instruments when starting to make a choice about which one might suit your pocket and space as well as your child's level of commitment and preferred style of learning.

KEY TO SYMBOLS

The more ♪, the better the instrument suits a beginner. Those marked with a five, for example, will be relatively cheap to buy new, freely available second-hand, reasonable to maintain, light to carry and not too difficult to learn.

♪	Difficult
♪♪	Satisfactory
♪♪♪	Good
♪♪♪♪	Very good
♪♪♪♪♪	Excellent

(page references in parenthesis)	Purchase price new	Second-hand availability	Maintenance	Weight	Ease of Learning	Is a small version available?
STRING FAMILY						
VIOLIN (42–43)	♪♪♪♪♪	♪♪♪♪	♪♪♪♪♪	♪♪♪♪♪	♪♪	YES
VIOLA (44–45)	♪♪♪♪	♪♪♪	♪♪♪♪♪	♪♪♪♪♪	♪♪	YES
CELLO (46–47)	♪♪♪	♪♪♪♪	♪♪♪♪	♪♪♪	♪♪♪	YES
DOUBLE BASS (48–49)	♪♪	♪♪♪	♪♪♪	♪♪	♪♪♪	YES
HARP (50–51)	♪	♪	♪	♪	♪♪	YES
ACOUSTIC GUITAR (52)	♪♪♪♪♪	♪♪♪♪	♪♪♪♪	♪♪♪♪♪	♪♪♪	YES
ELECTRIC GUITAR (53)	♪♪♪♪	♪♪♪♪♪	♪♪♪	♪♪♪	♪♪♪	NO
BASS GUITAR (54–55)	♪♪♪♪	♪♪♪♪	♪♪♪	♪♪♪	♪♪♪♪	NO
SITAR (56–57)	♪♪♪	♪♪♪♪	♪♪♪	♪♪	♪♪	NO
LUTE (58–59)	♪♪	♪♪	♪♪	♪♪♪	♪♪	YES
MANDOLIN (59)	♪♪♪♪	♪♪♪♪	♪♪♪	♪♪♪♪♪	♪♪♪♪	NO
UKELELE (59)	♪♪♪♪♪	♪♪♪♪	♪♪♪♪♪	♪♪♪♪♪	♪♪♪♪	NO
BANJO (59)	♪♪♪♪	♪♪♪♪	♪♪♪♪	♪♪♪♪	♪♪♪♪	YES
BALALAIKA (59)	♪♪♪♪	♪♪♪♪	♪♪♪♪	♪♪♪♪	♪♪♪♪	YES

	Purchase price new	Second-hand availability	Maintenance	Weight	Ease of Learning	Is a small version available?
WOODWIND FAMILY						
OCARINA (62)	♩♩♩♩♩	♩♩♩♩♩	♩♩♩♩♩	♩♩♩♩♩	♩♩♩♩♩	YES
DESCANT RECORDER (63)	♩♩♩♩♩	♩♩♩♩♩	♩♩♩♩♩	♩♩♩♩♩	♩♩♩♩♩	NO
FLUTE (64–65)	♩♩♩♩♩	♩♩♩♩♩	♩♩♩	♩♩♩♩♩	♩♩♩	YES
OBOE (66–67)	♩♩♩♩	♩♩♩	♩♩♩	♩♩♩♩♩	♩♩♩♩	NO
CLARINET (68–69)	♩♩♩♩	♩♩♩♩♩	♩♩♩♩	♩♩♩♩♩	♩♩♩♩	YES
BASSOON (70–71)	♩♩♩	♩♩♩	♩♩♩	♩♩♩	♩♩♩	YES
SAXOPHONE (72–73)	♩♩♩♩	♩♩♩♩	♩♩♩	♩♩♩	♩♩♩♩	NO
BRASS FAMILY						
CORNET (76–77)	♩♩♩♩♩	♩♩♩♩	♩♩♩♩	♩♩♩♩	♩♩♩	NO
TRUMPET (76–77)	♩♩♩♩♩	♩♩♩♩	♩♩♩♩	♩♩♩♩	♩♩♩	NO
FRENCH HORN (78–79)	♩♩♩♩♩	♩♩♩♩♩	♩♩♩♩♩	♩♩♩♩♩	♩♩♩♩♩	NO
TROMBONE (80–81)	♩♩♩	♩♩♩♩	♩♩♩	♩♩♩	♩♩	YES
TENOR HORN (82)	♩♩♩	♩♩♩	♩♩♩	♩♩♩	♩♩♩	NO
TUBA (83)	♩♩♩♩	♩♩♩	♩♩♩	♩	♩♩	NO
BARITONE HORN (84)	♩♩♩♩	♩♩♩	♩♩♩	♩♩♩	♩♩♩	NO
EUPHONIUM (85)	♩♩♩♩	♩♩♩	♩♩♩	♩♩	♩♩♩♩	NO
PERCUSSION FAMILY						
DRUM KIT (90–91)	♩♩♩♩	♩♩♩♩♩	♩♩♩	♩♩♩♩	♩♩♩	YES
STEEL PANS (92–93)	♩♩♩	♩♩♩	♩♩♩	♩♩	♩♩♩♩	YES
DJEMBE (94)	♩♩♩♩♩	♩♩♩	♩♩♩♩	♩♩♩♩	♩♩♩♩	YES
TABLA (95)	♩♩♩♩♩	♩♩♩♩	♩♩♩♩♩	♩♩♩♩	♩♩♩	YES
KEYBOARD FAMILY						
PIANO (98–99)	♩♩	♩♩♩♩♩	♩♩♩	♩	♩♩♩	YES
ELECTRONIC KEYBOARD (100–101)	♩♩♩♩	♩♩♩♩♩	♩♩♩	♩♩♩	♩♩♩	YES
HARMONIUM (102–103)	♩♩♩♩	♩♩♩	♩♩♩	♩♩♩	♩♩♩	YES
HARPSICHORD (104)	♩	♩	♩	♩♩	♩♩	NO
ORGAN (105)	♩	♩♩	♩♩♩	♩♩	♩♩♩	NO
TRADITIONAL INSTRUMENTS						
FIDDLE (108)	♩♩♩♩♩	♩♩♩♩	♩♩♩♩♩	♩♩♩♩♩	♩♩♩	YES
CONCERTINA (109)	♩♩♩♩	♩♩♩♩	♩♩♩♩	♩♩♩♩	♩♩♩♩	NO
ACCORDION (110)	♩♩♩	♩♩♩	♩♩♩	♩♩♩	♩♩♩	YES
PIPES (111)	♩♩♩	♩♩♩	♩♩♩	♩♩♩	♩♩♩	YES
HARMONICA (112)	♩♩♩♩♩	♩♩♩	♩♩♩♩♩	♩♩♩♩♩	♩♩♩♩	YES
FOLK HARP (113)	♩♩♩♩	♩♩♩	♩♩♩	♩♩♩♩	♩♩♩♩	YES

GLOSSARY OF TERMS

Accompaniment

A pianist may play the accompaniment in a sonata for violin and piano. An orchestra may play the accompaniment in a concerto for clarinet.

Alto

The lower pitched mature female voice. The term is also used to denote instruments of certain pitch ranges in instrumental families, for example, alto saxophone and alto flute.

Baroque

Refers to a period in the arts from about 1600–1750 and the style that dominated that period. Bach and Handel were Baroque composers. The word derives from the Portuguese.

Bass

The lowest sounding mature male voice. The term is also used to denote instruments of certain pitch ranges in instrumental families, for example bass clarinet and bass trombone, and is used to refer to the lowest part in a harmony.

Bass clef

Sign placed at the beginning of a stave (five lines and spaces on which music is notated). It indicates which pitches are to be associated with each line and space.

Bore

In brass and woodwind instruments, this is the name given to the tube into which air is blown (literally, it is the hole in the centre of the instrument). Instruments either have a cylindrical bore, for example the clarinet, or a conical bore, as in the saxophone.

Chromatic

In Western music the smallest pitch interval between notes in terms of instrument design and construction is thesemitone. A chromatic scale is one which moves up or down one semitone at a time. Within an octave there are 12 semitones.

Classical

Refers to a period in the arts from about 1750–1830 and the style that dominated that period. Beethoven, Haydn and Mozart were Classical composers. The word is often used to denote 'serious' or non-popular music.

Concerto

Most commonly used to define a piece of music for solo instrument, usually with orchestral accompaniment. The solo concerto developed in the Classical period.

Concert pitch

Concert pitch is A440, often written A=440 Hz. This means that on a piano the note A above middle C is tuned to 440 Hertz. This pitch was standardized in 1939. Prior to this date, individual instrument makers worked to the pitch they preferred. The need for standardization accompanied the rise of the orchestra in the 19th century and the increased mobility of instrumentalists.

Conservatoire (conservatory)

A music conservatoire is a music school or college where students work to a very high standard. The Royal College of Music and Royal Academy of Music in London are conservatoires.

Consort

Used to describe a group of instruments. A whole consort denotes instruments from the same family; a broken consort comprises differing instruments.

Dynamics

Describes the range of volume in a piece of music, or its performance, or attainable by an instrument.

Embouchure

The shaping of the mouth and lips to accommodate and play a wind instrument. The correct embouchure allows a musician to play the full range of an instrument without straining facial muscles.

Ensembles (see box, page 119)

Glissando

A continuous slide from one pitch to another.

Harmonic series

When a column of air or a single string vibrates, it is said to produce its fundamental note. In fact, the string or air also vibrates simultaneously in smaller portions, each producing one note in what is termed the harmonic series. It is the relative strength or weakness of the harmonics produced by a given instrument that gives it its characteristic sound or timbre

(for example, it is what makes an oboe sound different to a clarinet or a violon sound different to a cello).

Orchestra (see box, page 119)

Orff, Carl

German composer and music educator best known for Carmina Burana, written in 1937, and for developing the Orff Schulwerk (Music for Children) teaching methodology. This method, with its use of classroom percussion instruments, allowschildren access to composition, improvisation and other musical skills.

Perfect pitch

The ability to recognise a note by its pitch name without having another note to which to reference it.

Phrasing

Western classical music is composed and played in phrases, rather like the clauses in a sentence, which may be indicated by phrase marks in the notation.

Pitch

A musical sound has a given pitch. Each key on a piano plays a note of a particular pitch.

Plectrum

A device for plucking or strumming some stringed instruments, for example, the guitar.

Practice

An essential part of learning to play an instrument. There are no short cuts and daily practice is advisable.

Relative pitch

Relating one note to another. When given the name and pitch of one note most musicians can identify the name and pitch of a second note in relation to the first.

Romantic

Refers to a period in the arts from about 1850–1920 and the style that dominated that period. Brahms and Tchaikovsky were Romantic composers.

Sonata

A form in instrumental music that developed in the Baroque period and is most commonly associated with the Classical era.

Soprano

Describes a high-pitched female mature voice and is also used to denote instruments of certain pitch ranges in instrumental families, such as the soprano saxophone.

Stave

The five lines and spaces upon which music is notated.

Suzuki

A twentieth-century Japanese music educator who developed a teaching method that emphasizes the development of aural skills in advance of music-reading skills.

Symphony

An extended composition for orchestra, usually in several parts, or movements. The word comes from the Greek and means 'a sounding together'.

Tenor

Describes a high-pitched male mature voice and is also used to denote instruments of certain pitch ranges in instrumental families, for example, the tenor trombone, tenor saxophone and tenor horn.

Timbre

The quality of a musical sound that distinguishes it from another sound. For example, the timbre of an oboe makes a note sound different from a note of the same pitch played on a clarinet.

Transposition

Trumpet, French horn and clarinet are examples of instruments which produce sounds that are transposed, or different from the written notation.

Treble clef

Sign placed at the beginning of a stave (five lines and spaces on which music is notated). It indicates which pitches are to be associated with each line and space.

Ensembles

A musical ensemble is any group of two or more musicians gathered together to play music. These can take many forms and are known by different names according to their size and composition.

Brass band

A musical ensemble consisting principally of brass instruments with some percussion.

Band

Any musical ensemble.

Military band

Comprised of instruments played by soldiers. A military band is capable of playing music for ceremonial occasions and can play while marching. It includes woodwind, brass and percussion instruments.

Orchestra

A musical ensemble that usually includes string, woodwind, brass and percussion instruments.

Recorder consort

A group of recorders including instruments across the whole range of the family, from the high-pitched sopranino to the low-pitched great bass. The term is associated with the heyday of the instrument in the 16th century, although it is still applied today.

Recorder group

The modern version of a recorder consort, which may not include as many members of this family of instruments. Most schools have a recorder group or recorder ensemble rather than a consort.

String quartet

Four members of the string family: two violins, one viola and one cello. Each plays a separate part and the violins are identified as first and second. The first violin is the leader of the quartet and the part written for this instrument will, overall, be of higher notes than the second violin part.

Wind quintet

Four members of the woodwind family and one brass instrument. The standard wind quintet comprises flute, oboe, clarinet, French horn and bassoon.

Windband

An ensemble of woodwind, brass and percussion instruments, which can range from 40–80 players and is the equivalent of an orchestra, but without strings.

concert pitch 116–17
concertina 109
concerto 116
conservatoire 117
consort 117
    recorder consort 119
contracts with schools or agencies 20
coordination skills 34
copyrights 27
cornets 76–7
costs and maintenance 25–6, 36
    cleaning 27–8, 36
    see also under individual instruments

D
descant recorder 63
djembe 94
double bass 48–9
drum kits 28, 90–1
dynamics 117

E
electric guitar 53
    learning styles 14–15
electronic keyboards 100–1
embouchure 117
ensembles 13, 15, 20–1, 119
euphonium 85
exams 29

F
festivals 29
fiddle 108
flute 64–5
folk music 107–13

accordion 110
concertina 109
fiddle 108
folk harp 113
harmonica 112
pipes 111
string instruments 41
forcing children to learn 11–12
French horn 78–9

G
glissando 117
glockenspiel 88
group lessons 19
group/team player personalities 35
guiro 89
guitars
    acoustic 52
    bass 54–5
    electric 14–15, 53

H
harmonic series 117
harmonica 112
harmonium 102–3
harp 50–1
    buying music for 27
    folk harp 113
harpsichord 104
Highland bagpipes 111
home lessons *see* individual lessons
horns
    baritone 84
    French 78–9
    tenor 82
hygiene 27

ACKNOWLEDGEMENTS

Author acknowledgements

I am grateful to the many friends and colleagues who gave me help and advice with the preparation of this text.

About the author

Richard Crozier taught in secondary schools as Head/Director of Music for many years, and also worked as a woodwind teacher and Area Music Coordinator in the County of Avon. In 1991 he was appointed County Music Inspector in Bedfordshire and this was followed by time as an Ofsted-trained inspector of primary and secondary schools. In 1995, Richard moved to the Associated Board of the Royal Schools of Music as Course Director for the CT ABRSM (Certificate of Teaching, Associated Board of the Royal Schools of Music).

Richard is past Chair of the National Association of Music Educators, past member of the editorial board of the *British Journal of Music Education* and current member of the board of the Pictorial Charts Education Trust. He is the author of *Offbeat*, a practical guide to pop and jazz for GCSE, and co-author of *Carousel*, a primary music scheme, and, with Paul Harris, *The Music Teacher's Companion*. He is co-project director of *All Together!*, a book about group teaching.

Executive Editor Jane McIntosh
Editor Lisa John
Executive Art Editor Penny Stock
Typesetter Dorchester Typesetting
Production Manager Ian Paton
Illustrator Sudden Impact Media